"Alison and I drove the Jasp afternoon of the accident. It was surreal. But he was not in the van with us. We left him at the hospital with a sheet over his little body. From those moments forward, I had a front row seat to this family's reaction to the tragedy that had befallen them. Although experiencing soulful anguish few of us can even imagine, they stayed true to God and never wavered in their faith in Jesus Christ. This book will be a true inspiration to anyone who reads it."

– TIM WILDMON, *president, American Family Association/ American Family Radio*

"I cannot imagine any person who would not benefit from this inspiring story. We need to know: God turns sorrow into hope. We need to know how God uses tough times to shape our character. The Jasper family is proof. This book is worth your time.

– MAX LUCADO, *New York Times best-selling author of* You'll Get Through This

"God bless J.J. and Melanie Jasper for sharing their story to be a spiritual encouragement to so many others who have suffered unbearable loss. We highly recommend *Losing Cooper: Finding Hope To Grieve Well.*"

– RICH BOTT, *president, and* DICK BOTT, *founder, Bott Radio Network*

"There is no greater pain than losing a child. Craig and I know that personally, as do J.J. and Melanie Jasper. But, the Jaspers know something else – that even in the midst of the most devastating loss, we can know God's sweet gift of mercy, unexpected peace, and abiding love. Read how the Jaspers' loss reminded them once again of our great gain through Jesus."

– JANET PARSHALL, *host/executive producer, "In the Market with Janet Parshall"*

"God often brings the greatest stories of comfort, healing, and re-demption out of the toughest tragedies. I've heard this unbelievable story firsthand and am so glad it is now in print for us to share with others. Use this powerful resource as a reminder that the glory of Christ often shines brightest through our broken places."

— STEPHEN KENDRICK, *author of* The Love Dare *and producer of* **Courageous**

"Although Christians are not immune to grief, we do not have to grieve 'As those who have no hope.' Every Christian who has ever felt the sting of death from the loss of a loved one – or knows someone who has – will be wonderfully encouraged by *Losing Cooper*."

— DR. ROBERT JEFFRESS, *pastor, First Baptist Church, Dallas, Texas*

"Unimaginable is the only word to describe the tragedy of losing a child. Undeniable is the only word to describe the faith of J.J. and Melanie in dealing with the loss of Cooper. As a front row observer to the moments and days immediately following the accident, I can tell you that what is written on these pages is a genuine testimony to the power of hope. This story is not about selling books but about sharing hope. In a moment everything in the Jaspers' lives was shattered, but hope remained. That hope has a name – Jesus!"

— JEFF ULMER, *pastor, New Life Family Church, Biloxi, Mississippi*

"Most people rail out to God when they face a tragic loss, but when their five-year-old son, Cooper, was taken in an accident, J. J. Jasper and his wife, Melanie, asked God to help them grieve well. Their poignant story is full of victory and hope, and will encourage anyone who's suf-fered soul-deep pain. I highly recommend this book."

— TERRI BLACKSTOCK, *author of* Truth Stained Lies *and* Distortion

"*Losing Cooper* is a deeply moving story of how two of our most treasured friends faced the worst tragedy parents can imagine, yet they did so without losing each other or their trust in God's boundless grace and mercy. We, along with countless others, have been greatly inspired by J.J. and Melanie Jasper's endurance and we're confident that all who read this skillfully written story will be inspired by it as well."

— STEVE AND ANNIE CHAPMAN, *singers/songwriters and best-selling authors*

"If you have ever dealt with the grief from a great loss or have desire to minister to someone who has suffered loss, this is a must read. If you need to understand the importance of God's presence in one's life of faith, this book is a necessity. I know you will be moved to a closer relationship with the Lord as *Losing Cooper* ministers to you through God and the courage of Melanie and J.J."

— DAN CELIA, *president/CEO, Financial Issues Stewardship Ministries*

"Christianity is unique in its ability to inspire hope. Among the world's faith systems, Christianity alone can legitimately promise that believers will have a joyful reunion in heaven. For followers of Jesus, promises about God's care here and hereafter are tangible realities!
"Few stories communicate these truths as clearly and effectively as *Losing Cooper.* The gripping story of the Jasper family and their walk through a valley of unimaginable depth will move and inspire every reader. I highly recommend this book that uses a true story to vividly display the power of Jesus."

— ALEX MCFARLAND, *founder, Truth For A New Generation apologetics conferences*

"This inspiring family's story has been life changing to many. Their transparency brings healing and hope in the midst of such a deep loss. This book teaches real life principles on the importance of grieving well and clinging to Jesus. A powerful read for all walks of life!"

– SARAH REEVES, *singer/songwriter*

"I've seen what God has done in people's lives with the movie **Flame On**, providing hope to the hopeless and a lifeline to those in the pit of despair. I've also seen J.J. praying over the pages of this book, asking God to use each word, his family's testimony, and Cooper's story to provide healing to those who are grieving. I believe God has answered that prayer."

– RON SHANK, *program director, American Family Radio*

"'Mr. Brother Kevin,' that is what Coop called me. That means I am close enough to the Jaspers to confirm two things: One, Cooper was every bit a special boy as described in this work. And two, the Lord God was every bit as faithful and powerful to help the Jaspers grieve well when they were ambushed by grief. No matter what you have been through in your life, the words of this book will give you courage and point you to Christ to help you...grieve well."

– KEVIN MANGUM, *pastor, River Point Community Church, Cornelia, Georgia*

"This is the story of a real family facing real tragedy and finding that a real God is enough in the deepest and darkest places of this life. J.J. and Melanie allow us into their family's journey to answer the questions of where is God and who is God when our lives fall apart? So find a quiet place and a good cup of coffee because you are about to experience what Jesus meant when He said, 'My grace is sufficient for you, for My strength is made perfect in weakness.'"

– TONY KARNES, *pastor, Michael Memorial Baptist Church, Gulfport, Mississippi*

"Cooper, well, he was a precious gift straight from God from the very beginning. He was everything his daddy and mommy say he was… and then some. He was that kid. He always wanted to help. He never forgot a face. And he smiled one-hundred percent of the time. Cooper loved to have fun, yet he was so kind-hearted and sensitive. Everyone loved Cooper and he loved everyone even more. He loved being around people but no one more than his own family. I'll never forget the time Melanie brought him over while she went to a doctor's appointment. He said good-bye, gave her enough kisses and hugs to last a whole week, then just as we were about to walk into the house he darted back for just one more.

We had the extraordinary privilege of knowing and loving Cooper. Every week he greeted us with a high-five, superhero style! The Jaspers' heart is to acknowledge that nobody is immune to life's tragedies, yet there is hope in the aftermath from the daily ache of grief and loss. This book is for those who have experienced or know someone who has experienced great heartache, to discover that there is hope no matter what the circumstances. We have seen J.J. and Melanie's suffering lead them straight to the heart of God, and they aspire to share that ultimate hope with others."

– STEVE TYBOR, *president and co-founder, Eight Days of Hope*

LOSING COOPER

Finding Hope to Grieve Well

✣

J.J. JASPER

To B.J & Brandy
God Bless you!

[signature]

Cover and interior design by Rusty Benson

All quotes from the Bible are from New International Version unless otherwise noted.

ISBN (Hard cover version) 978-0-578-14190-9
ISBN (Soft cover version) 978-0-578-14196-1

Printed in the United States of America by Signature Book Printing, www.sbpbooks.com

Brett Morgan Publishing, P. O. Box 804, Tupelo, MS 38802

www.jjjasper.com

DEDICATED TO

The memory of Samuel Cooper Jasper,
the most remarkable boy I have ever known.

CONTENTS

ACKNOWLEGMENTS

The first person I want to thank is my Lord and Savior Jesus Christ. I love Him because He first loved me. I am so grateful to God for my wonderful wife, Melanie, and my beautiful daughters, Lauren, Sadie Morgan, Maddie and Kasie James.

Melanie, thank you for all of your hard work, input, and support of this project. Thank you for writing the most moving chapter in the book! Lauren, thank you for writing your chapter as well – you are a gifted communicator.

I'm grateful for Rev. Don Wildmon, Tim Wildmon, and the entire Wildmon family. Thank you for your leadership, influence, and friendship. This project would not be possible without the help of American Family Association and American Family Radio.

Special thanks to Ed Vitagliano. Besides Melanie, no one has worked harder or contributed more to this book. Thank you, Ed, for your constant encouragement, editing, and for all the chapters you "tweaked."

Special thanks to one of my dearest friends, Randall Murphree, for insight and editing. Randall, I'm indebted to you for the countless Saturdays you sacrificed and for your treasured friendship.

Special thanks to Rusty Benson for cover design, layout, editing, and more!

Thank you, Stephen Kendrick, for coaching and encouragement.

Thank you, Errol Castens, for your valuable contribution and your friendship.

Thank you, Stacy Long, for editing.

Thank you, Debbie Fischer for transcribing.

Thank you, Optimus Media@optimusmedia.com for web design and I.T. consulting.

I'm grateful for the coaching and encouragement that I receive daily from Ron Shank and Travis Haley.

Thanks to my friend and pastor, Scooter Noland, for your prayers, support, and influence in my life.

Thanks to my friend, neighbor, and co-pilot, Jim Barton. I've enjoyed every one of our many flights together except one – the time the engine quit and we had to make an emergency landing on the highway!

When thanking people who have helped in significant ways, you always run the risk of leaving someone out. I am so thankful for family, friends, church members, co-workers, and especially our wonderful radio family who listen to AFR. Thank you for your kind comments, prayers, and support over the years.

God bless you,

J.J. Jasper

Foreword

Every Sunday morning began the same in the small trailer park in which I grew up. My dad would give me a couple of quarters and tell me to head to the laundry mat on the corner where I was to buy a newspaper. As a boy, I looked forward to reading the Sunday paper. I would grab the paper and go for the section right in the middle of the paper, normally nestled next to all the coupons and sales advertisements. There, I would find my treasure, the comics! I looked forward to reading all of the comic strips; but my favorite was "Peanuts." I would root for Charlie Brown to finally get to kick the football that Lucy was place-holding. Each time the comic strip ended in the same way. Lucy would pull the ball away from Charlie Brown at the very last second, and he would go flying through the air as he exclaimed, "Good grief!" It sounds like an oxymoron. "Good grief." Is there such a thing? Can grief really be good? Can it produce anything good?

If you have experienced loss or pain, then you may be familiar with some of the more popular verses about grief:

"Let not your heart be troubled; you believe in God, believe also in Me" (John 14:1).

"I have told you these things, so that in Me you may have peace. In this world you will have trouble. But take heart! I have overcome the world" (John 16:33).

"Consider it pure joy, my brothers and sisters, whenever you face trials of many kinds, because you know that the testing of your faith produces perseverance. Let perseverance finish its work so

that you may be mature and complete, not lacking anything"
(James 1:2-4).

When we think of grief, we automatically think of people in the Bible like Joseph, Job, and David. We know that just about all of the heroes of the faith experienced grief of some kind and in some way. Surely at the top of the list of suffering people we can find Jesus. Isaiah writes,
"He was despised and rejected by mankind, a man of suffering,
and familiar with pain.
Like one from whom people hide their faces He was despised, and
we held Him in low esteem.
Surely He took up our pain
and bore our suffering,
yet we considered Him punished by God,
stricken by Him, and afflicted.
But He was pierced for our transgressions,
He was crushed for our iniquities;
the punishment that brought us peace was on Him,
and by His wounds we are healed" (Isaiah 53:3-5).

Jesus, the Savior of the world, familiar with our sufferings? What a thought!

The people and the pages of Scripture have much to say about grief. After all, the Scriptures were written by the One whose only Son was murdered by the very people He created. After Jesus was crucified, He returned to His disciples and astounded them that He was alive. Upon His return, He appeared to the disciples and hundreds of others. The sorrow they experienced over His death was now alleviated knowing that He was alive, and they had witnessed his appearance personally. However, He was about to leave them again. He promised the Holy Spirit would come in His absence, to comfort them, guide them, and fill them with His power. Jesus then returned to heaven, again. So the Bible speaks to both the experience of human suffering and the healing of God's comfort.

As J.J. and Melanie's pastor, I can tell you that this book is written by an authentic Christian couple who experienced the devastating death of their only son. It is full of practical and Biblical insights to offer help and healing to anyone who needs hope. Suffering through Cooper's death, the Jaspers know what it's like to hurt, to have unanswered questions and to experience any parent's worst nightmare. But they also know how God can turn a tragedy into triumph and bring beauty from ashes. This should be on the bookshelf of every grieving family."

— Scooter Noland
Lead Pastor, Hope Church
Tupelo, Mississippi

Introduction

After the death of our five-year-old son, Cooper, the first few days and weeks were brutal. The horror and shock, denial and sense of loss are indescribable. The pain was overwhelming. We seemed to be in a fog those first few weeks and much of that time is blurry. I do remember, however, Melanie and I spent much time sobbing uncontrollably and holding each other close. It was very difficult to even breathe. When we would catch our breath, between shoulder-shaking sobs we would pray a simple prayer: "Lord, help us grieve well." We weren't sure what that meant or what it looked like, but we all know of stories where someone lost a loved one and they plunged into alcohol or drug addiction or their marriage failed or they were paralyzed with debilitating grief that seemed to shut them down completely. We desperately did not want to go off the deep end. We desired to glorify God even in our pain. We were clinging to the Lord for the sake of our marriage, our Christian testimony and our own mental health. Plus, our other children needed us, and we needed to be strong and stable for them.

We were frantically hanging on for dear life trying to stay sane and not wanting to become a statistic of a ruined life. I can tell you that the pain is so cruel and so constant that it's understandable to me why people collapse completely under the weight of the grief. The pain of having your child die is so indescribably intense that there is surely no chart or graph to measure it.

However, we thank God and praise His holy name that His grace is sufficient and He does provide help and hope. He hears and answers prayers. We were able to make it through the worst day/days of our lives, and we believe God gave us strength to grieve well. That explains the subtitle of this book. This is not a comprehensive guide on how to grieve. One of the many lessons we've learned through this journey is that everyone grieves differently. However, there seem to be stages of grief, and we learned some things that helped and some things that hurt, and we simply want to offer insight and share our story. It's a story of pain and loss, but the bigger story is about a God who loves you and can sustain you.

For you to be reading this, I'm assuming that you've lost a loved one or know someone who has. Please know that no matter how dark the tunnel or how deep the pit you find yourself in, there is hope. If you are hurting, there is a healer who can help. His name is Jesus of Nazareth. He is the Lamb of God that takes away the sin of the world, He is the Rose of Sharon, the Lily of the Valley, the Bright and Morning Star. He is our high priest who was tempted in every way just like we are, but without sin. He was a man of sorrow acquainted with grief. He is close to the broken-hearted. He has promised never to leave us or forsake us. If you will allow Him, He will hold your hand and walk with you every step of the way on this difficult journey. If you've lost a job, your marriage or like us, lost a loved one and you're desperately wondering if you'll make it through this...the answer is yes! With God's help you can and will make it. You can make it because of the precious blood of Jesus that was shed for you, the promises in His holy Word and through the Holy Spirit of the living God. If you are grieving today, it is our prayer and God's promise for you to grieve well.

Do not be far from me, my God;
come quickly, God, to help me.

PSALM 71:12

Suddenly

Do you remember where you were Friday afternoon, July 17, 2009? I'll never forget. That was the day our only son, five-year-old Cooper, died in an accident on our family farm.

The previous day had been wonderful. I had just returned from a business trip to Denver. I was missing my wife and kids immensely. It was so good to return home Thursday afternoon, collect all the hugs and kisses, and pass out the little souvenirs. Ours is a close-knit family, and even a trip lasting only a few days is met with a rousing, "Daddy's home!" and lots of love. Often the greetings came complete with a handmade "Welcome home" banner. One of the many things that I appreciate about my wife, Melanie, is how she orchestrates events like that to always show me love and respect and teach our children to do the same.

Friday I had to go to work but hurried home afterward, so excited to see my wife and children. Even though our oldest daughter, Lauren, was away at church camp, the rest of us were together, the weather was beautiful, and the weekend was here! Everything seemed perfect in our little world.

Since Melanie had been managing all alone with the children for the past five days I insisted she take a break and go into town. We needed a spark plug for the push mower and she had some errands to run so she reluctantly went to Walmart alone. The plan was I would mow our yard on the riding lawnmower with our son, Cooper, riding on my lap while two of our children stayed indoors. We started mowing but soon the mower quit. After our efforts to restart it failed, we decided to hop on the swing set for a while in our back yard.

Cooper then went around to the front yard to gather up a bunch of plastic wiffle balls the kids had been playing with the day before. He emerged from the front yard with an arm full of balls and a huge smile on his face and announced: "Momma will be so happy when she gets home and sees how I've cleaned up the yard." Cooper was a unique boy in that he loved to serve and seemed filled with joy when he was being helpful.

With his mission accomplished, he then started to ride his bike around in circles in the garage. Melanie had just put his training wheels on the bike that day and he was so proud of his bike and new wheels! He alternated between riding his bike and the two of us swinging on the swing set. I was having as much fun as he was.

Then I suggested that we ride our dune buggy. He was actually content riding his bike but after some urging he agreed. We rode up and down the dirt lane across our pasture. I slowed way down without saying anything, then looked over at Cooper to get his reaction. He looked puzzled as to why we had almost stopped, looked up, grinned really big, and yelled, "Flame on!"

"Flame on," was an expression from one of Cooper's favorite super-heros – the Human Torch. A team member of the Fantastic Four, the Human Torch could burst into flames, but not be consumed by the fire. Because the Torch used the words "Flame on" to ignite his super power the expression became a favorite of Cooper's. "Flame on!" meant "Go faster!"

This game continued. I would slow down to a crawl, Cooper would laugh hysterically and yell, "Flame on!" Then I would gun it and race down the dirt road on a straight stretch in our pasture. While we were playing this impromptu game, I remember thinking how we had not said a word but just exchanged glances, with him squealing out, "Flame on," to make me go faster. I remember thinking how wonderful it was that we loved each other so much and knew each other so well that we had made up a game, established the rules, were having so much fun together, and all without saying anything except Cooper's favorite expression! It is so amazing to be that close to someone that you can exchange glances and just by the look in his eyes know what to do and even what he's thinking. It's strange the things I remember from that fateful day.

After we played this game for several trips down the lane, I thought I should head back to the house to check on our girls. I decided to turn the wheel, floor it and do what we always called a "doughnut" growing up. It's where you spin the back-end of a vehicle around, then continue on straight. The area in the pasture was level, Cooper was buckled in, and we were riding in the safest off-road vehicle we could purchase. It had a full roll-cage, padded side roll-bars and was very low to the ground with a wide stance. I turned the wheel, floored the accelerator, and the back-end started to spin around, but then something went terribly wrong. The dune buggy flipped over.

I was not buckled in so the rollover threw me out, but I was unhurt. Immediately I glanced over at the dune buggy lying on its side with Cooper still securely fastened in his seat belt. I got up and raced to his side thinking, *If he has a scratch on him or if somehow his little arm is broken, I'll never be able to forgive myself.*

Then the unthinkable unfolded and we experienced every parent's worst nightmare. Cooper didn't have a scratch on him, but the rollover had broken his little neck. On July 17, 2009, our only son died in my arms on our family farm.

It happened that suddenly.

Obviously, we never planned to write this book. Our plans, like other parents, were to watch our children grow up, get a good education, and accomplish their dreams and goals while serving the Lord all the days of their long lives. However, in an instant, our dreams were destroyed. Our entire world as we knew it came crashing down around us. It is profoundly true what they say about how your whole life can completely change in only an instant. There really are no words to describe the overwhelming, catastrophic pain of losing a child. It has been agonizing, cruel, and dark. At times we felt we were just teetering on the edge of a precipice, dangerously close to plummeting into despair or a paralyzing pain that would rob life of any joy or meaning.

God was with us, however. He is faithful and was there for us, and He will be there for you if you're hurting. Jesus was victorious, conquering death and the grave. There is everlasting hope! That is why we wrote this book, to tell our story and offer hope that is only found in the Lord.

Popular Bible teacher Beth Moore has said:

But make no mistake, when we are in the driest desert, we can receive the manna to make it all the way to the other side where trees bud again and children laugh. God sometimes delivers us from evils we never see. Other times, He says, "When you pass through the waters, I will be with you; and when you pass through the rivers they will not sweep over you … Do not be afraid, for I am with you; I will bring your children from the east and gather you from the west." (Isaiah 43:2, 5) [1]

This book isn't mainly about us or Cooper, it's about a faithful God who created you and loves you. He knows everything about your circumstance and situation and He can help. We have sensed His presence throughout our journey. Because of the truth of God's Word and the power of His Holy Spirit and the power of prayer, we are still standing. Those of you who have lost loved ones know you can't make it in your own strength. A pain this deep and this intense requires supernatural help. Jesus led us out of that dark valley, and He has been there every painful step of the way.

We have not completely escaped the darkness. Certainly there are still times of agony and pain. Sometimes, seemingly out of nowhere, we get ambushed by grief. We miss Cooper desperately. We dream of his smile and hear the sound of his laughter echo in our hearts. His absence has left a jagged wound that will never fully heal. But the Lord is there for those times, too. And He will be there for the suffering you are enduring or will endure. One day all His children will be together again, with no tears or suffering or sorrow to separate us.

If you are hurting, we want to try to offer help and hope in these pages. We want to comfort you with the comfort and help that we've received. In fact, the Bible says, "Praise be to the God and Father of our Lord Jesus Christ, the Father of compassion and the God of all comfort, who comforts us in all our troubles, so that we can comfort those in any trouble with the comfort we ourselves have received from God," (2 Corinthians 1:3-4).

Certainly, we don't pretend to know how you feel or how deeply you're hurting. We don't know your story or where you are in this journey. Now that we are several years down the road, we want to humbly offer perspective or insight that's been helpful to us to hopefully help you.

Please don't give up. Don't stop. Don't give in. Please don't throw in the towel. Continue to breathe and just try to make every effort to put one foot in front of the other. Then get up tomorrow and do the same. With God's help you can do this. Author and pastor Max Lucado puts it this way: "You'll get through this. It won't be painless. It won't be quick. But God will use this mess for good. Don't be foolish or naive. But don't despair either, with God's help, you'll get through this." [2]

The boundary lines have fallen for me in pleasant places;
surely I have a delightful inheritance.
PSALM 16:6

2

Our Story

Every journey starts somewhere, and mine began in Owensboro, Kentucky, where I was born and raised. I moved to Tupelo, Mississippi, when I was in my 20s. The Lord opened the door for me to make a career change from construction to broadcasting. I started my broadcasting career at Christian radio station WCFB and after five years there, was invited to work with the American Family Association. Since 1991 I've been a morning on-air personality with the American Family Radio network, which has approximately two hundred stations in 36 states.

With so many radio stations, there is a lot of travel involved representing AFR to our listeners. I enjoy public speaking and actually do stand-up comedy many weekends across the country. I met my wife Melanie in October 1997 through the connection of her mother, Kandi Anderson, who was working as an on-air talent at WAOY, one of our radio stations, located in Gulfport, Mississippi. Kandi is a regional Bible teacher on the Mississippi Gulf Coast, a speaker for women's events, and a columnist for the local newspaper.

I was scheduled to do a night of comedy at Michael Memorial Baptist Church in Gulfport, teaming up with Christian singer/songwriter, Kelly Willard. WAOY upped the ante and held a contest where the winner could meet Kelly and me at a fish-fry. The dinner was at the home of Kandi and her husband, Lowry.

As a private pilot always looking for a chance to fly, I rented an airplane and flew from Tupelo to Nashville, Tennessee, to pick up Kelly. But we were delayed in Nashville, needing a mechanic to check out the plane because the landing gear wasn't working properly. Because of the delay, we were a little late arriving at the fish-fry. The Andersons' back yard was transformed into a coastal paradise. They had a real gift of hospitality, and whether it was working with youth, entertaining friends or hosting a Sunday school party, they always did it up right. Tables lined up beside the pond were filled with an assortment of delicious food, guaranteeing an afternoon of great food and fellowship.

Almost immediately I noticed Melanie. She actually brought me iced tea and we chatted briefly. Those of you who are more sensitive to the Holy Spirit will understand what happened next. It seemed that the Lord spoke to my heart for me to make sure and have my antenna up regarding Melanie. I wasn't sure what that meant, but it was a very clear nudge from the Lord to pay attention. Other times in the past, when the Lord would give me a similar nudge about a particular person, before the day was over there would be a divine opportunity to counsel them or share the gospel. I assumed that was the case here since I didn't know anything about Melanie.

As the fish-fry wound down and we all got in various vehicles to go to church for the music and comedy event, I just followed and climbed in the nearest available car with Kelly and some others. When the driver of the car climbed in I wasn't surprised that it was Melanie. It seemed that the Lord was speaking to my heart to "pay close attention because I'm doing a work regarding this young lady." It's fun to watch these "coincidences" unfold as a person follows Christ. Whoever said, "It is dull and boring to be a Christian," was wrong. Attempting to live a spirit led life is exciting! It's incredibly rewarding and it's an amazing adventure. Oddly enough, during the ride to the church, Kelly did all of the talking.

After the concert everyone headed to a local restaurant for coffee and dessert. Eventually, Melanie and I did get to talk. As we laughed and talked, it was comfortable and seemed as if we had known each other our entire lives. Before the evening was over it got almost eerie because we were finishing each other's sentences and would exchange glances like we knew something very special was taking place right before our eyes. Maybe "love at first sight" is an over-used phrase, but for lack of a better description that's what happened on that wonderful evening. It certainly didn't hurt that Melanie was a gorgeous, strawberry blonde with a great personality and an obvious love for Jesus. That night I was so convinced she was the one, that I called my best friend, Kenny, in Kentucky to tell him I just met the girl I was going to marry. That was pretty ironic because Kenny and his wife, Paula, had been trying to get me married for a decade and were convinced that I'd let a lot of good ones get away. Of course, unknown to me, Melanie had called a friend of hers and had almost the exact conversation that I had with Kenny.

Melanie had a two-year-old daughter from a previous marriage. Although Melanie had remained faithful and exhausted every avenue to save her marriage, it ended in divorce. She had moved back home with her parents and was trying to make ends meet as a single mom. She was seeking the Lord with her whole heart and trusting God for her future. After our "love at first sight" encounter, Mel and I enjoyed a long distance relationship racking up huge phone bills, but we certainly got to know each other better and grew closer. We both had suffered broken hearts with dating situations in the past, and neither one of us wanted to play games or waste each other's time. So early on, we prayed for God's direction in our relationship. We did not want our feelings for each other to go beyond what God intended only to have our relationship end in disappointment and heartache. Trying to wisely guard our hearts and seek the Lord's will, we actually fasted and prayed diligently before too much time was invested. Our love for each other grew, and after much prayer and confirmation, I proposed! I'm old fashioned so I did ask Melanie's dad for permission to marry his daughter, and then I proposed to her on bended knee.

We had a beautiful church wedding attended by family, friends, church members and radio listeners on Saturday, May 2, 1998, in Tupelo, Mississippi.

Two pastors, Rev. Oda Shouse and Steve Hallman, shared the duties at our ceremony. When the traditional wedding march music began, the guests all stood, and the most beautiful bride ever entered the sanctuary. Steve started the wedding in traditional fashion asking, "Who gives this bride?" and received the response from Melanie's dad. As he continued through the typical ceremony, he suddenly stopped and said, "Since this is such a serious service, I've given lots of thought and prayer to what I would say. I want my words to count. I want to say the most appropriate thing that will carry the most weight and have the maximum impact. I've really struggled to find the right words to begin this wedding ceremony, and I believe I know what I'm supposed to say." After such an intense wind-up there was a hush over the crowd, and you could have heard a pin drop in the church.

Steve then leaned forward and said, "Melanie, it's not too late to back out!" Everyone erupted with laughter and believe me, we never saw that coming! I'll have to say, it was the perfect ice-breaker that seemed to settle nerves and cause everyone to relax and enjoy the ceremony. Plus, Melanie can't say she wasn't warned! Laughter has always been a big part of both of our lives, and it seems to show up everywhere! Laughter really is good medicine.

Family has also played a huge role in both of our lives. I married into a wonderful family. My father-in-law, Lowry, was in the lumber business for 30 years and was very active in lay ministry. He eventually surrendered to the call of ministry and became a full-time pastor with God using him mightily. You've heard the old saying, "When God made him, he broke the mold." That was the case with Lowry. He was a true original: smart, athletic, and entertaining with a very unique sense of humor. Because Melanie grew up with her dad's zany antics it made the transition to my similar brand of humor seamless.

Lowry had so much joy and was such a bundle of energy. Allow me to illustrate. I forget which holiday it was, but we had all of the family over, and we were enjoying good food and fun. There was a high level of noise, laughter, and energy, which was pretty typical for our bunch. There was a suggestion for some of the men to go to the store to pick up some needed items. Suddenly, there was a lull and everything got really quiet. Because it had gotten so calm, we asked, "Where did everyone go?" We quickly realized that only Lowry had gone to the store! When he left a room, it was as if three or four people were gone. That's how much excitement and fun he brought to every situation. Lowry passed away March 14, 2008, after a short battle with cancer. He was truly an amazing man who seemed larger than life. He is profoundly missed by everyone who knew and loved him.

After Lowry passed away, Kandi remarried and God blessed her with Cooper Farris, a fine Christian man. Cooper's wife had also died of cancer and the Lord was faithful to bring this "Hall of Fame" coach into Kandi's life. Besides being an award winning baseball coach he is a man of character and integrity.

Melanie's younger brother, Zach, is a decorated Marine. He was a door gunner on a Huey helicopter and was among the first wave that went into Afghanistan after 9/11 and then was in Iraq for the "Shock and Awe" operation of Iraqi Freedom in 2003, the beginning of the long war in Iraq. Zach is a committed Christian and a dedicated family man. He is one of the most naturally gifted athletes I've ever met. He is a police officer in Tupelo, and logged considerable time with the SWAT team there. Zach's beautiful wife, Tiffany, is equally athletic and talented. When you meet them, you quickly understand the many "Ken and Barbie" references made about this dynamic couple.

Kasie, Melanie's only sister, is a beautiful wife and mother. Besides being sisters, they are best friends. She is a gifted singer and talented hairdresser. Jeremy, Kasie's husband, is an associate pastor/youth pastor and is one of the most well rounded men you'll ever meet. There are many great role models in Melanie's family, and it is a blessing to see how many are actually involved in various ministries.

On my side of the family, I also have a lot of wonderful, talented relatives. My mom and dad both passed away in 2011. Dad was one of the smartest men I ever knew and was quick witted. Mom was amazing. Martha Jasper, was kind, gentle, loving, patient, and one of the most thoughtful people you'd ever meet. She was an avid reader, a threat to unsuspecting crossword puzzles, and very intelligent. She was the valedictorian at her school.

I was probably seven or eight before I knew my mom was handicapped. A neighborhood boy inquired about my crippled mother. Crippled? All I knew up until that point was that she was the prettiest girl in the whole wide world, and she was my mama. Sure enough though, Mom was handicapped. She had a hereditary neuromuscular disorder that primarily affects the feet, legs, and hands. It is a severe form of muscular atrophy. Mom struggled to walk and had limited use of her hands. I guess I never realized it; however, because she worked 40 hours a week, raised four kids all born within six years – and never complained. My mother had a difficult life with many obstacles, but she never let her handicap prevent her from doing anything. Strong, resilient and brave, she was a survivor. I don't think we show our moms the love and appreciation they deserve. The one who carried us for nine months, changed our diapers, sat up rocking us when we were sick, cooked, cleaned, and hauled us around like a taxi service, and all the many other thankless things moms do. God did some of His best work when He created mothers.

My brother, Mike, was the oldest and may have been the smartest and most talented among us. He suffered from several addictions, however, never realized his full potential, and died from cirrhosis of the liver in 2004.

Kelly and Karen are my two younger sisters. Kelly is a beautiful wife and mother and nearly an exact replica of Mom. She is one of the kindest, most thoughtful people you will ever meet. Karen, our youngest sister, is also a beautiful wife and mother. Karen is hardworking, loyal and hilarious. All who know her agree that she could be a stand-up comedian. My brothers-in-law are terrific along with our many nephews and nieces. We are certainly blessed with a wonderful family. Melanie was a great fit and was welcomed into our family with open arms.

Scripture teaches, "He who finds a wife finds a good thing" (Proverbs 18:22, NKJ). My beautiful bride, Melanie, is smart, witty, athletic and a hard worker. She is an awesome wife and mother and really does exemplify a Proverbs 31 woman. God blessed me in more ways than I can explain by allowing us to become one flesh. She is such a loving, Godly woman. I can't imagine life without her. I'm so grateful to be on this journey married to my best friend, the love of my life!

After Melanie and I married, her two-year-old, Lauren and I hit it off. I actually wrote an entire chapter about Lauren in 2001 in my book, *Moses was a Basket Case*. Here is how I described her:

> If Dennis the Menace and Shirley Temple married and had a child, she would be just like our Lauren. My wife, Melanie, claims Lauren is three little boys wrapped up in a little girl's body. She is completely at home playing in a dirt pile with a frog in each hand or a pretty dress singing up on stage in front of an audience. No one meets Lauren and forgets her. Some people have the personality of a clenched fist. Then there are those like Lauren: bright, bubbly, relishing every moment of any situation. I have never in all my life met anyone more alive. When Lauren exits a room, she leaves a wake.
>
> Make no mistake – she is fun but also fiercely independent. Lauren is the poster girl for the strong-willed child. We jokingly said a good website address for her would be www.getdownfromthere.com.

When Melanie and I married, I actually got two for the price of one. Melanie had Lauren from a previous marriage. Lauren was two years old when we married. After the wedding, they moved in, and I was amazed at the energy a toddler possesses. After the first couple of hours of witnessing this demonstration of perpetual motion, I thought, *This has been fun. Can we just take the batteries out, put her up on a shelf and get her down another day?*

I quickly learned it doesn't work that way. I found out that Lauren only operated on two settings – on or off – and just two speeds – full throttle or total collapse. She was wide open and into everything, and always giving 100%, but this was brand new to me. Those of you with tiny tykes know exactly what I'm talking about. Whether it's a jaw-dropping, wide-eyed enthusiastic response to a butterfly sighting or the gusto in eating a a simple meal, with food flying in every direction – in the floor, on her face, in her hair – it's all or nothing. Have you noticed when preschoolers get tickled, they laugh all over themselves? When they throw a fit, it's "Katie, bar the door 'cause they're not taking any prisoners." No matter where they are when they throw a fit – if it's in the grocery store or church aisle – it's a doozy.

Those of you with little ones know how sincerely they live their lives. There's not a fake bone in their little bodies. I just hoped I would be on the right side of the learning curve. After being a bachelor for so many years, I suddenly found myself a husband and a father on the same day. As a microwave dad, I had – and have – lots to learn.

Lauren and I became fast friends. We had an instant rapport. On her own, she started calling me "Daddy." I'm convinced there is not a sweeter sound than to hear the word "Daddy" spoken from the lips of a little one. "Hold me, Daddy, I'm cold." "Hug me, Daddy, I'm scared." All the demands and stresses of the workplace dissolve when you hear that wonderful moniker spoken with a slight baby lisp. Is there a sweeter sound than to hear, "Daddy's home! Daddy's home!"? I never would have guessed so much pure love could be packaged so small, and I never dreamed you could have so much love for someone so tiny. Hot tears have made more than one slalom run down the ski slopes of my cheeks when I realized how undeserving I am to share in the love of this child.

I'm not trying to win a "Dad of the Year" contest, but it has been a high priority for me to make time to do things together with Lauren. We try to build things, read books, tell stories, go on daddy and daughter dates, etc. Lauren and I have fished and flown airplanes, we've wrestled in the floor and laughed until we cried. We've put diapers on our heads and danced together (long story). I once let her cut my hair with real scissors (an even longer story). I never knew how much fun these little people could be. As a parent you get a marvelous front row seat to rediscover the simple joys of life. What a thrill to view life from a child's eyes.

We enjoyed a charmed life. Our life revolved around lots of love and laughter, travel, ministry, and special times with family and friends. Each year we were one of the dreaded families that sent out the syrupy sweet Christmas newsletter highlighting the ways the Lord had blessed us throughout the year. Yes, I know those newsletters are nauseating to some, but I actually enjoy getting them to see how good God is to others. We packed a lot into a few short years. Mel and I built a cabin on a lake (where we still live) and we did much of the construction ourselves. We had a baby nearly every year for several years.

Eventually Melanie and I had four more children together. Sadie Morgan, Maddie, Cooper and Kasie James. We are so proud of our five children, and they bring us immeasurable joy. We do everything together, and whether at work or at play, they are a constant reminder that children are truly a gift from God.

Our close-knit extended family is a gift, too, which has played an important role in our children's lives. It is a blessing for Melanie and me to watch one of our kids and spot a family trait from parents, a favorite uncle, sibling or grandparent. Part of the wonder and joy of having your own children is to see how heredity and genealogy play such a large role in shaping them. We're grateful for the influence and heritage that our combined families bring to the table to shape who our children are and what they will become.

Because we are a close-knit family, Cooper's death left a massive hole that spanned several generations.

Now we find ourselves in foreign territory, this tear saturated place of grieving the death of one of our children. It is a place so awful, terrible and unnatural that there is not even a name for this new role that was thrust upon us. It has been noted that someone who has lost a husband is a widow. A child whose parents died is called an orphan. But, has it every occurred to you, there is no title for parents whose child has died.

Behold, children are a heritage from the Lord,
the fruit of the womb, a reward.

PSALM 127:3 (ESV)

3

Children

As I mentioned, when Melanie and I got married, we were an instant family, but we immediately planned to have additional children. Things did not go according to our plans, however. Many months passed and Melanie hadn't conceived. We started to have concerns about whether or not I could father a child. Melanie had Lauren, so surely the disconnect was on my end. Those of you who have wrestled with infertility issues know the drill. You get your hopes up month after month only to have them dashed by false alarms. Many months of discouragement were made worse for me due to my male ego "macho" concerns.

There were seasons when we would stop trying to get pregnant and then just not do anything to prevent it. Months turned into years in our struggle with infertility. I finally agreed to a doctor's appointment with a fertility specialist. Let me say that, as a man, embarrassment is not a strong enough word regarding this process. Humiliation is a better description.

Any couple who wants to have a child of their own but is unable to see this desire fulfilled, no doubt experiences a roller coaster of emotions. Some couples accept what they believe to be God's plan for their lives and receive the grace necessary to live victoriously. Others adopt children and find fulfillment as parents, bringing joy to the lives of those who are chosen. In our case we were very grateful for Lauren and were trying to accept the realization that our happy little home might include just the three of us.

Meanwhile, during the three years we were trying to get pregnant, we continued to make church a big part of our life. We have always tried to be faithful and take part in all that our church has to offer. Our local church where we have been long-time members had small groups that seemed to add to the feel of "community" you experience when you are plugged into a local body of believers. It's a way to fellowship with other families on a more intimate level, and accountability is there. We were part of a small group that took turns meeting in each of our homes, and the families in our small group were wonderful. We experienced a real closeness and great fellowship that centered around Bible study.

One Sunday night we were meeting in our home. We had enjoyed great singing and teaching, and we were concluding our small group time by taking prayer requests. Several in our group were expecting babies. Someone asked in a light-hearted way when we were going to add to our family. Oddly enough we had not shared our struggle in this area with the sweet, precious brothers and sisters in our small group. I suppose we were just suffering in silence. Isn't that the way it goes sometimes? The obvious ones to whom you should reach out for prayer and support, you fail to ask.

Well that night after it was brought up, we shared our desire to have a baby. We told our story of disappointment. Beverly, one of the ladies in our group boldly recommended that Melanie sit in a chair and suggested that everyone lay hands on her and pray according to promises in Scripture that God does indeed hear and answer prayer. Melanie willingly sat in the chair. The group gathered around her and placed their hands on her head and shoulders and lovingly prayed for her by faith in Jesus' name, believing God at his word.

And speaking of prayer, over the years, little Lauren would ask repeatedly for a sibling to play with. Melanie would explain that all good gifts come from God and that she should pray. Many times Lauren would be busy playing in the living room floor with her toys and abruptly stop what she was doing, close her eyes, clasp her little hands together, and pray, "Lord Jesus, please give me a little sister." This same process was repeated over and over. Lauren prayed earnestly for a baby sister.

We met several weeks later at our Bible study small group at Johnnie and Suzanne Long's home. Imagine our surprise when Johnnie said to Melanie with a smile on his face, "Melanie, you're pregnant."

"No, I'm not," Melanie answered.

Then he matter-of-factly replied, "Yes, you are. The Lord told me to tell you that you are and that *she* is going to be a blessing."

Melanie had only told one person that she thought she might be pregnant and that was her friend Amy. Amy had even brought a pregnancy test to Melanie that evening for her to take the next morning. Melanie proceeded to tell Johnnie that she had her suspicions that she was and was going to take the test Amy had brought to her.

He said, "Take it if you want to, but call me after you do and tell me I was right." Which was exactly what happened the next day! Praise God from whom all blessings flow. So, about three weeks from the time Melanie was prayed over, we found out we were expecting! We chose not to find out the gender of the baby, but we certainly pondered in our hearts all that surrounded this incredible answer to prayer including Johnnie's words that *she* was going to be a blessing.

Sadie Morgan Jasper, a baby who was longed for and prayed for, was signed, sealed, and delivered on March 14, 2001. Because I am on the radio every weekday morning, our lives have been lived out before our wonderful listeners, so Sadie was born with much fanfare. We had so many emails congratulating us, and there was a record number of people in our room at the women's hospital after she was born. And oh, by the way, she is a blessing!

When we were deciding on a name for Sadie, Melanie mentioned that her great-grandmother's name was Sadie. She had fond memories of her. She was sweet and kind and had a wonderful sense of humor.

I loved the name. It was a name from the past, beautiful and unique. I suggested we name our daughter after Melanie's great-grandmother and use both her first and middle name. After asking Melanie what her great-grandmother's middle name was she wasn't sure if she had ever heard it. So, she asked her mother who didn't know either.

Now, the element of mystery had come into play. It was a game – a treasure hunt! I was getting very curious at this point to discover the mysterious middle name so we could name our Sadie. So, Melanie called her Grandaddy Frank, to find the answer.

"Oh, you're wanting to know your Grandma Sadie's full name? Well, it was Sadie Earl Key." Whoa! Earl, a middle name for a girl? Boy, I thought, *Back in the old days they sure had some unusual names didn't they?* But Melanie and I were not naming our sweet little girl Sadie Earl, we just couldn't do it! We decided on Sadie Morgan. After all that effort, Sadie's middle name wasn't from a relative or a friend. It was just a name that I saw in the newspaper and liked. When I mentioned it to Melanie, she loved it, too. And as is common in the South, we call her by her double name as often as not. There are a lot of interesting stories about family names, aren't there?

After Sadie was born, the Lord blessed us with even more children. (More about them later.) He is able to do exceedingly more than we can ask or imagine. Almost before we realized it, Lauren – (then eight) had three siblings ages one, two and three. Can you imagine? I would jokingly say, "With a one-year-old, two-year-old, three-year-old and an eight-year-old, there was a lot of crying at our house ... and sometimes the babies were crying, too!" Or I'd ask, "Do you know that diaper spelled backward is rcpaid?" There was always lots of noise and activity in our home, but our children brought us so much joy, and it was worth it! And after all, we had prayed for it! Our lives seem to revolve around our children much like parents everywhere.

Because I married late in life, family and close friends were convinced that I would be a lifelong, confirmed bachelor. I shudder to think I almost missed out on the blessings that children bring. Please allow me to say, if you have longed for children to no avail, I certainly don't want to add insult to injury regarding your situation. I want to be sensitive to that hope. I'm just trying to make the case for how wonderful family life is – if that's God's will for your life.

Someone once said having children is like living in a frat house – everything is broken, nobody sleeps, and there's a lot of throwing up! We laugh at that but sometimes I'm concerned that the secular world around us has that view about children.

To be one hundred percent honest, when I was single, even as a committed born again Christian, I viewed children as spoilers in a way. I would watch members of the singles community get married and seem to be put "out of commission." As I would quiz my friends about married life, more often than not I would hear the old "ball and chain" line about marriage complete with unpleasant stories of constant nagging, all of the expenses, and their limited freedom.

Then when children came along I heard my old friends complain about children being "spoilers." I would hear these same stories about friends building race cars, or attempting to get a pilot's license, or how close they came to realizing their dreams of a sports career, and these stories all had a common denominator. Kids came along and spoiled everything.

In subtle and often not so subtle ways, here is what was communicated to me: "You can't have any nice furniture if you have kids." "I was in great shape until I had kids; having a baby ruined my figure." "You can't get ahead because having children is so expensive."

My friends would say, "I had to abandon my dreams because of a wife and kids."

Married people, be careful! Many of you are doing a lousy job of representing family life to your single friends.

I'm a people person, and I've been told my whole life that I've never met a stranger. I do love to meet people, talk to them and hear their stories. Years ago when talking to "transplants," folks who had moved to my town from another area, there was a surprising trend. Many would explain that they sold their business, quit their practice or opted for early retirement, sold everything, and moved clear across the country. When I quizzed them as to why they would suddenly pick up their roots and make such a radical move, the answer was almost always the same: "To be near our grandchild who was recently born!" As a single guy with no kids, I'll admit I didn't get it but there was no denying it even then; there must be something very special indeed about little ones that would cause so many people to make such a major move just to be close to the grand-kids, to be able to spend more time with them. Back then, I didn't understand how wonderful children are but I do now.

Kids aren't spoilers! God's word says this: "Sons are a heritage from the Lord, children a reward from Him. Like arrows in the hands of a warrior are sons born in one's youth. Blessed is the man whose quiver is full of them" (Psalm 127:3-5a). When my wife and children came along, that's when my life started! I didn't have to abandon my dreams; children are the best thing that's ever happened in my life. I love being happily married with kids! My wife completes me! It's awesome and I want to shout it from the rooftop!

The secular world says children are a burden and a bother and they're constantly in the way. I like God's opinion of children better. He says children are our heritage. Children are a blessing and a reward from his own hand. If you have children, almighty God looked down, smiled on you and rewarded you. I'm thankful beyond words for how blessed I am to be a dad! As parents, we get naming rights. We have a front row seat to watch these precious babies who are pure and innocent. They have such a zeal for learning and such a zest for life. We are able to be kids again as we see life through their eyes. I can't put a price tag on how much it's meant to put my arm around Melanie and peek in on our sleeping newborn babies. Their hands and feet are so tiny, and their skin is so soft. And who can resist the giggle of a small child. I remember especially when our children were young, I would come home tired at the end of a long day at work and one of the kids would yell, "Daddy's home!" They would all stampede down the hall and surround me. Instantly the cares of the day would melt away.

Yes, children are expensive, and sure they are noisy, and they do have sticky fingers – oh, but they're worth it! I'm amazed at how the Lord is able to pack so much into such a tiny package.

For you created my inmost being;
you knit me together in my mother's womb.
I praise you because I am fearfully
and wonderfully made;
your works are wonderful.
I know that full well.

PSALM 139:13-14

4
Pro-life

I love the story told of a little girl fascinated by her new baby cousin. She asked her mother, "Can't we please have a baby?"

"I don't believe so, darling," her mother replied. "They cost too much."

"How much?" the child inquired.

"Oh, about ten thousand dollars," her mother said.

The daughter thought for a moment, then said, "That's not very much, when you consider how long they last."

In the Bible we read, "My frame was not hidden from You when I was made in the secret place. When I was woven together in the depths of the earth, Your eyes saw my unformed body. All the days ordained for me were written in Your book before one of them came to be" (Psalm 139:15-16).

You are precious in the sight of God and were created in His image. You have value! You are not an accident. You were made by God and you are loved by God.

By now you can tell that I'm definitely pro-life. I'm convinced that January 22, 1973, was a sad day for America. In the *Roe v. Wade* decision, Supreme Court Justices voted 7-2 that the constitution gives us the right to shed innocent blood. Today in the United States, nearly every third pregnancy ends in abortion. Every year, more unborn children die from abortion than Americans died in the Revolutionary War, the Civil War, World Wars I and II, the Korean, Vietnam, and Persian Gulf wars combined. God help us. Please pray for the holocaust of abortion to end.

All life is precious in the sight of God, from conception to natural death.

If you have had an abortion, please know that this is not an attempt to judge or condemn you. Please realize that God's grace and forgiveness are available to you. You can be healed and completely forgiven. God wants to help you, restore you and make you whole.

However, I make no apology for believing in the sanctity of human life. In fact, to my skeptical friends, I sometimes ask two questions about those babies in the womb. If it's not human life, what life form is it? If it's not alive why is it growing? I've been privileged to be the keynote speaker at many pregnancy resource centers' banquets and I sometimes quote Steve Farrar from his book *Point Man:*

> Before I married, I used to have a BMW. I had a lot of fun with that car. I now have three kids and no BMW. I have an Audi that's eight years old with more than 100,000 miles on it. Hundreds of M&M's are crushed into the fibers of its carpet, and teenage mutant Ninja turtles lurk under the seats. When my daughter Rachel was three, she crawled up on the front bumper of my two-month-old car and sketched a picture on my hood with a rock. Her artwork is still there.
>
> My BMW used to be flawless. With three kids, my Audi is anything but. Yet my life has greatly improved. God has brought more blessing into my life through these three children than any material possession ever could. Trust me. It's a lot more fun raising kids than BMWs.
>
> Psalm 127:3 is right. Children are a gift from the Lord. May He reward you with them! My wife and I have been blessed by three little lives that have given us more joy than all of the travel, gourmet food, BMWs, and designer clothes that the Gold Card can buy. May God bless you with as much joy! And may you be smart enough to recognize a good deal when you see it. And, by the way ... as long as you're going to have one, you might

as well go for two, three or four. I know you can't afford it. But you'll sure have a great time. You'll also be very tired. But that's all right. You can rest in heaven. [3]

I've noticed that conversations about pro-life topics seem to evoke passionate feelings from both sides of the debate.

We were surprised and disappointed about how many negative comments we heard even from the Christian community, when we announced that Melanie was pregnant with our fourth child, Cooper. We heard sarcastic remarks like, "Don't you know what's causing that?" and, "I'm glad it's you and not me." Even some family members voiced concerns that we were making a mistake by having more than three children. Large families used to be the norm, but in our modern society they seem to be frowned upon.

During this time I was talking with a youth minister friend on the phone. Halfway through our conversation I mentioned we were expecting again. My friend seemed troubled by this news, and she began to gently scold me by saying, "What were you thinking? How are you going to pay for college and weddings for so many children?" She continued the rebuke by saying, "Kids are fine and good, but you have to use common sense, God gave us a brain; there is no way you can afford to have another child." Our conversation shifted to the upcoming event that we were both participating in. Just before saying goodbye I asked her, "Hey, can I ask you a hypothetical question?"

"Sure," she said.

"What if you were contacted by an attorney who discovered that a long lost rich uncle that you weren't even aware of died and left you five exotic luxury vehicles. A Lamborghini, a Maserati, a Porsche and two others. What would your response be?"

She laughed and said, "Are you kidding? I'd be ecstatic!"

I continued, "How would your family and friends react?"

She cheerfully responded, "They would say, 'Whoo hoo! Congratulations. Good for you. You are so lucky, we're jealous!'"

Then I set the hook and asked, "Do you know how much repairs are for a Lamborghini? Do you have any idea how high taxes, insurance and tune-ups are for a Porsche? Why are you excited? What are you thinking? God has given you a brain. There is no way you could possibly afford all those luxury vehicles, even if they were given to you."

There was only silence on her end of the phone. In radio it's called "dead-air." She finally spoke and simply said, "Touché." There was another pause and she meekly confessed, "I guess it's really what we place value on isn't it? Maybe we are all mixed up in the things we think are important." She then thanked me. Actually until that moment I had never thought of that scenario. It had just come to me as an illustration of the worth of children as we were talking.

I can tell you this much about having lots of children, there is never a dull moment at our house! Once, when it was only the three of us, we took our eyes off Lauren for only a couple of minutes and it had gotten a little too quiet. You parents know that usually means trouble. Lauren was three years old at the time. Let me remind you that Lauren was very smart. Probably too smart for her own good and too big for her britches. There seems to be one in every family, and Lauren was very precocious.

After a quick search we found her in the kitchen floor eating out of a tub of chocolate ice cream with the freezer door wide open. She was covered from head to toe in chocolate. Can you picture that? She was holding the tub of ice cream with her feet like a chimpanzee and using a serving spoon which was nearly as big as her head. You could see her eyes and her smile but everything else was mostly chocolate – and she was sitting in a puddle of chocolate on our solid white floor. Lauren was a gooey, sticky mess.

I went off on her, "You're not supposed to get in the refrigerator! And look, you've left the door wide open! And look at the sticky mess you made! Who's gonna clean this mess up?"

After I paused to take a breath, Lauren looked up and said, "Daddy, you need to take your burdens to the Lord and lay them down." She was holding the big spoon like a pointer, chocolate dripping from her elbow, and she continued, "You need to take your burdens to the Lord and lay them down, and when you do, you need to leave them there!"

Amazing! Hilarious, and pretty good advice from a three-year-old. Lauren is all grown up now. She is smart, beautiful and very talented. She is a gifted writer and an amazing singer. She is a college student, and we are very proud of what the Lord is doing in her life.

All of our children are artistic and good with crafts, but Sadie is truly an artist. For as long as we can remember, she has been focused on drawing and art. She carried a sketch pad with her as a child and for a while even went to bed with an Etch-a-sketch! When you have artistic types in your home, they can be very unpredictable. I'm trying to be very diplomatic here, but musicians and artists seem to march to the beat of a different drum.

Once, when Sadie was about four or five years old, I came home from work and she was sitting on the couch reading one of those thick paged children's books and eating potato chips from a bowl next to her. She was holding a pair of cooking tongs. She was turning the pages of the book with the tongs and getting the chips out of the bowl and putting them in her mouth with the tongs. I stopped mid-stride to observe this clumsy process.

I asked Melanie, "What's with the tongs?"

She replied, "Beats me! As soon as she woke up this morning, she declared, 'Today I'm not going to use my hands.' She brushed her hair with the tongs, brushed her teeth with the tongs. She dressed herself completely using only the tongs. She has nearly gone the entire day true to her mission of not using her hands!"

That's our little artist, Sadie. She's also a talented drummer, softball player and a straight A student just to name a few of her talents. Everyone seems to have fun stories of their own children especially when they were small.

Maddie is our third child. Maddie is a talented gymnast, very athletic, and she has a servant's heart. She is one of the sweetest, kindest children you'll meet. She is also a hard worker. Once, when Maddie was little, we were at church on a Sunday morning. The service had concluded and people were leaving the sanctuary. Several of us couples with small children lingered in the back enjoying an extended time of fellowship. As we talked, our children laughed and played on the first few rows in the front of the church. We had enjoyed each other's company so much that we lost track of time. A few of the couples suggested that we should probably be leaving and we all looked to the front of the church to begin rounding up our little ones.

Just then Maddie broke from the group and made her way to the altar. She knelt down, bowed her head and closed her eyes. She placed her sweet face in her hands and began talking in a whisper. All of the couples oohed and aahed, and Melanie and I held hands. *It's working,* we thought. You bring your children to church, you try to raise them right, and occasionally you get to see a glimpse of the reward. Just to see this sweet precious cherub going to the altar on her own was very moving.

Until she got louder. She raised her head and started shouting, "Eight, nine, ten, ready or not here I come!" And then she took off running. Oh, my, our children keep us humble don't they? They have us on an emotional roller coaster. You are up and excited, then down you go with a good dose of reality. Maddie is so much fun and a tremendous blessing.

Once I came into the kitchen and Cooper was on all fours eating from a pile of brown stuff on the floor. Our youngest two girls were standing guard. When I immediately showed concern. Sadie said, "Relax, Daddy. Those are just Grape Nuts. It's our sweet feed and Cooper is our cow. We're playing cattle farmer!"

Just then Cooper reached out with his hand and they scolded him, "Hey we've already told you cows don't eat with their hands!" Cooper plopped his hands flat on the floor and continued bobbing for the "sweet feed." With Grape Nuts on his face and the way he would moo occasionally, I'll have to say the Grape Nuts looked like sweet feed and Cooper made a pretty good cow! As I mentioned, there's never a dull moment at our house!

The latest addition to our family is our baby girl, Kasie James. She was born June 30, 2010, almost a year after the accident that claimed Cooper's life. The story surrounding Kasie James was a very private and personal one – until now. After Cooper died, we were at our lowest point in our grief. We were in the early stages, and the pain was still very raw. Certainly all we could think of was Cooper. Every minute of every day our thoughts were consumed with images of our little boy. It seemed like we would have to pry our minds away from thoughts of Cooper being gone just to get any day-to-day practical things done. It was like a movie that plays over and over in your mind, a film about the life of your loved one intermingled with a longing to see and hold him that human words cannot express.

In the quiet moments between tears, Melanie and I certainly reflected on what's really important. Thoughts of life and death, the uncertain future, and our children would consume us. During this time somehow the possibility of having another child made its way into our conversation. We were smart enough to know that we could never replace Cooper and also cautiously aware that our desires could be fueled by our grief. After someone you love dies, it seems you have a sharper focus on what is really important and what's going to last. When you think about what's valuable on this earth, the worth of a child, a living breathing person, is certainly on the top of the list.

However, it's wise immediately after a death not to make any big life-altering decisions because you are unstable and may not be thinking clearly. Although we weren't taking prescription medications in order to cope with our grief, we know that many families do, and that could certainly affect decision making.

Being cautious wasn't our only concern. There were a lot of things that discouraged us from thinking about having another child. We had actually tried to have another baby when Cooper was small, but our last two pregnancies had ended in miscarriage. Because of that, we had assumed that having more children wasn't the plan. Yet the thought of another baby seemed to be on our minds a lot.

There were other things to be concerned about, too. One was my age. I am several years older than Melanie and was in my 40s when Cooper was born. I wondered if I would have enough energy to keep up with another baby, and I wanted to be around long enough to see our children marry and have families of their own. Also, I have rheumatoid arthritis and take some pretty potent medication to keep it at bay. We felt it would be necessary for me to discontinue taking the medicine while we were attempting to conceive so as not to affect the baby's health. (The medicine is actually a low-grade chemo-therapy.) If I'm negligent and miss a few days of the arthritis medicine, the pain is almost unbearable.

So there we were, facing some discouraging realities. Were we making a decision based on emotion? Is having another child at my age fair to the baby? And can I go several months without the medicine? (This would be a good time for you ladies to weigh in and say it's actually past time for a man to endure some physical pain associated with childbirth!) What if this pregnancy ends like the last two? The pain from a miscarriage on the heels of the death of our baby boy would surely be more than we could bear.

Well, you already know the decision we made. We chose life. Babies are so important to us and have brought so much meaning and value to our life that we consider the reward to outweigh the risk. Certainly, this is our personal decision, and each couple has their own story, but I can't tell you what an amazing, beautiful, incredible baby Kasie James is! We can't remember what life was like without her. She has brought so much additional love and joy into our home. In fact, consider this wonderful pro-life testimony, that while we were at the lowest point in our family's history, just the thoughts of her being on the way buoyed us and gave us hope. Looking forward to the day she would be born gave us a glorious distraction from the pain with which we were otherwise consumed. I would cradle Kasie James in my arms when she was a newborn and whisper to her, "Before you were even born God used you in our family's life. Before you drew your first breath or even saw the light of day, He used you in a mighty way to give us more hope and joy than any other source." I can't wait until Kasie James is a young lady and we can communicate to her how God used her in our life at our lowest point.

Have I mentioned how beautiful she is? She looks just like her mother and is so full of personality. Like our other children, she is smart, very busy, and effervescent. Kasie James is a very special gift from God, and she brings a smile to nearly everyone who meets her. Once while we were on vacation we announced to the children that we would head down to the kiddie pool at the hotel where we were staying. With unbridled enthusiasm Kasie James shouted, "You mean they have a Hello Kitty pool!" I guess it goes without saying that we spent considerable time at the "Hello Kitty" pool that week on vacation. Whether it's her wide-eyed declaration of having just spotted a "runny babbit" or hundreds of other ways, she makes us laugh. Having her around is sometimes like having a raccoon loose in the house or like owning a chimpanzee. She is so very busy and almost an exact replica of Lauren when she was that age. Yes, children are a blessing. They are a reward and a gift from God's own hand. Every life is beautiful, from conception to natural death. Having children is worth it! Blessed is the man whose quiver is full of them!

Jesus said, "Let the little children come to me, and do not hinder them, for the kingdom of heaven belongs to such as these."

MATTHEW 19:14

5

Cooper

"It's time."

Any couple that's had a baby knows how much excitement, anxiety, and adrenaline those words evoke. You've prepared yourself as much as you can. The plan has been rehearsed and a backup plan is in place. The baby's room is ready. The bags have been packed for many weeks. You have a list of numbers so you know which family members and friends to call first with the news that you're on your way to the hospital to have the baby!

So when Melanie sensed that the baby was "here," and when she said it was time to have our son, we were ready!

Melanie and I already had three girls, so having a boy was going to be a new experience for us. Many people had naturally remarked, "So you're finally going to have a boy. You must be overjoyed." It's kind of funny though. If I had married in my 20s and someone had asked me if I wanted a boy or girl, like any red-blooded American male I would have said a boy. A son would be someone to play catch with or take fishing or hunting.

However, as a dad with *daughters* I found myself in a different mind-set early on in Melanie's pregnancy. Girls are incredibly special. Any father with daughters will tell you there is a unique bond between a father and his girls. Daughters know how to wrap Daddy around their little finger, but they also have the capacity of making Dad feel ten feet tall! So initially there was almost a slight reservation. I didn't want to change the dynamics or alter the chemistry of our family in any way.

Then again, it *was* only a "slight reservation." While I was perfectly content being a daddy to daughters, as the days grew near for the birth of our son, I got so excited. This was certainly going to be an amazing new chapter in our lives!

And then Melanie said the much anticipated words, "It's time," and the adventure began. We jumped in our vehicle, rushed to the hospital, and on our way, we called Mel's brother, Zach, a local police officer. Zach happened to be on duty and joined us en route to the hospital. So there we were, blue lights flashing with a police escort.

Samuel Cooper Jasper was born on February 24, 2004, at the North Mississippi Medical Center's Women's Hospital in Tupelo. He weighed 7 lbs. 14 ozs. We planned to call him Cooper even before he was born, but he was also known as "Coop."

He was born smiling, we used to say, and it's very nearly true. While he might not literally have come out of the womb with a grin on his face, Melanie spotted him smiling when he was only hours old and she mentioned it to me. And he spent the rest of his short life laughing and smiling.

Melanie would wake him up each morning and get him dressed. Then he would always get on her back and giggle all the way down the stairs. That was every single morning. It was just something Cooper and his momma did.

He rarely got upset. He was never in a bad mood. People think I'm making that up, but I'm not. Some people have said, "Well, he must have gone through the terrible twos." No, he by-passed all of that. He never, ever, stomped his foot and said no. Don't get me wrong: The rest of our kids were just like any others. They pitched an occasional fit, they stomped their foot and said no. This wasn't something special about Melanie and me; it was something special about Cooper, our little blonde-haired, blue-eyed boy with an adorable dimple.

He lived to be obedient. If you told him, "Stay right here and don't move," he would stay right there and starve to death. He would not disobey.

I leave for work very early, and Melanie would always say that Cooper woke up many mornings and said, "Mom, how can I help you today?" It brought him great joy to be obedient and helpful.

His heart was just so tender toward others. He was very aware of everyone around him. If someone looked sad, he would go check on them. He was very considerate and kind.

One day when he was four, he was with Melanie, who was visiting a friend at her yard sale. Melanie was sitting on the ground talking to some of the ladies, and she must have looked uncomfortable. Cooper found a little stool that was for sale and dragged it over for her. He said, "Here, Momma, this would be more comfortable."

All of Melanie's friends exclaimed, "Oh, my word! Even my husband wouldn't have thought to do that for me!"

That compassionate heart was always evident at school, too, even as a four-year-old. When he first started school, I remember one night at supper I asked him, "How did your day go today? Did you enjoy playing with your friends?" He answered that he didn't play with his friends. So I asked him why not, and in little boy words he said there was a new kid at school, and this new boy felt really left out and a little confused and scared. So Cooper had spent the last few days sitting with the boy and befriending him. "I didn't want him to be lonely or feel left out," he said.

Melanie told me one day the teacher told her something we'll never forget. The teacher had passed out papers to the students, and they were supposed to fill them out, mentioning their favorite color, the name of their pet, things like that. It was a little biography. Well, the teacher said that all the little boys in the class had put down Cooper as their best friend. Every single last one of them. But that was the kind of boy he was, even in grade K-4.

It wasn't just the other children that noticed this about Cooper. The adults noticed, too. The school he attended would give an award at the end of the school year for Best All Around – for one boy and one girl in the K-4/K-5 grades. It usually went to a K-5 student, but his teacher told Melanie and me, "We all knew it had to go to Cooper." It was the biggest award you could get in the entire school for his age.

Now, his sisters were always getting trophies for this or that, but he had never won a trophy. So, at this K-4 graduation he got his very first one. He was so excited. He held it up in front of the crowd and yelled, "Mom, Dad, my first trophy!" And, he kissed it. Everybody laughed. He kissed it and cradled it in his arms as he walked back to us. When he got home, he asked to take a bath with it, because he didn't want to part with it. (And yes we did let him bathe with his trophy!)

Even at a young age, Cooper was athletic, too, and extraordinarily strong. That wasn't too strange considering that Melanie and I were both active. I wrestled in high school and lifted weights. Mel played ball and spent a lot of time in the gym, so being strong is something we recognized.

When Cooper was a toddler, he got ahold of our push mower (It wasn't on, obviously!), and we saw him actually pushing the mower *uphill*. He was just a year old! His sisters would get in a wagon, and he would pull them around in it when he was not even two years old. He would lean back, get that thing moving, when he got some momentum going, his legs would start churning and he would lug them around the yard.

One day we were all out in the yard playing and all of a sudden we heard some grunting sounds. We turned around and saw that Cooper had fallen into a fire ant bed. He stood up, covered with the stinging ants. He had five ants on his lip alone – they were just hanging there stinging him. He never cried. It was like he was telling himself, "I can do this. I don't know what's happening to me, but I am going to power through this."

That was Cooper – compassionate and considerate and always smiling, but also bad to the bone!

But it was love that marked him more than any other characteristic. He was the most cuddly little guy. He would bury himself under your arm and he loved to be held. If you were sitting anywhere near him, he would come over and scrunch up to you. I would think to myself, "Doesn't he ever get hot, buried like that? Doesn't he ever get tired of doing this?" But he never did. You couldn't wear him down on the cuddling and you couldn't out-cuddle him.

His sisters loved him – and not just because he would pull them in the wagon! He was very smart and insightful, and sometimes his older sisters would be putting something together or working on a project and they would get stumped. And they would ask, "Cooper, can you help us with this?" He would stop what he was doing, go over there, take a look at it, identify the problem, put something together and help them. For instance, before he could even talk, Cooper taught himself to snap his fingers. His sisters, Sadie and Maddie, longed to do that but couldn't. And this toddler would waddle around smiling, snapping his fingers on both hands, almost gloating. He pantomimed and taught two of his three sisters how to snap their fingers. So, to this day when they snap their fingers they are reminded that a little guy who couldn't talk yet showed them how! They asked their little brother for advice all the time. He was our little problem solver.

But that was the way his mind worked. Cooper was a thinker and a planner even at a young age. I remember a few Saturdays when he would say, "Dad, I've been thinking. Today we could go to the zoo." (Or wherever.) He would continue to lay out the entire day and how it would unfold: "Mom can pack this and that, and while she is doing that, you'll have time to go and fill the Suburban up with gas and do the errands you said you needed to do today. You can get back at the same time that Mom will be finished, and we will be ready and we can go on this adventure."

Mel and I would glance at each other and agree that it was a good idea. Then we would all enjoy a family outing that a four-year-old completely planned! Can you imagine that? It may seem bizarre except that was so typical of Cooper. He really was a natural born leader.

He was extremely well organized for a boy his age. For example, he would always fold his pajamas up and put them back in the drawer as soon as he got up in the morning. There are so many things I could tell you about Cooper to emphasize how unique he was. His first word wasn't "Mama" or "Dada," his very first word was "backhoe!" At the end of a long day at bedtime, he would get up from the couch, stretch and say, "Guys, I think I'm going to call it a day. Do you mind if I go to bed?" He was certainly not your average child. It was World War III trying to get our other children to go to bed, but it wasn't unusual for Cooper to put himself to bed early. We had dozens of people say, "You know he never was a little boy. He went from being a baby to a little man."

While that was true in many ways, I don't want to overstate the case, either. Cooper was all boy, too, in wonder at the world around him. I remember I was always taking my pocketknife out and cutting strings on the hay bales as we put hay out for the cattle. I would let him use the knife with close supervision, and he started to ask me how old he had to be to get his own knife. So I went ahead and got him a knife but told him he couldn't use it until he was bigger. I got him a Swiss Army Knife and put it in his fishing tackle box.

It wasn't too long afterwards that Cooper came and told me, "It bugs me that it's down there in my tackle box and I can't see it." But I told him I didn't want him to get hurt. So he made me a counter-offer: "Well, how about this? Can we drive a little nail in the side of my dresser, hang it up there and when I'm lying in bed I can look at it? The first thing when I wake up, I can look over there and see my knife."

I told him we could do that but added, "You can't take it off that nail." He promised me he wouldn't, and he didn't. You couldn't make him break a promise. I hung that Swiss Army Knife on that nail and he would just lie on his bed, his hands behind his head, and look at his knife.

That's kind of how he acted toward the world around him, too. He was fascinated by everything. If I said to him, "Let's go outside and watch some paint dry," he would say, "All right!" He would put his red, rubber boots on and tell Melanie, "Daddy and I are going outside to watch some paint dry!" And he would thank me for including him. We would be out in our driveway which was brown gravel, and he would say to us, "Guys, look at this brown rock I found!" His enthusiasm was contagious.

Every experience was something for Cooper to enjoy. Melanie's sister, Kasie, a hairdresser, gave him his first haircut when he was only six months old. The first time I took him to the barbershop with me he was about nine months old. Most kids would be scared being in a strange place with a strange man cutting his hair, but he loved it.

I'll never forget that first haircut at the barber shop. The barber put him up on a board and was cutting his hair, and our little boy was all smiles. All the men were saying, "Wow! Every other kid screams and goes crazy." But that was typical Cooper. They were amazed that he was enjoying it, but he actually looked forward to getting his hair cut and would plead for Melanie to take him to get it cut regularly.

And as soon as he could talk, he insisted that Paul, one of the barbers at the barbershop, be the one to cut his hair, no matter how long the wait. And that was a bit strange, because Paul had long hair and a beard in contrast to the other barbers. If I were a little kid, I would have thought he was a little scary looking, but Paul was the one he was drawn to.

That love for life affected people. One day about a week before Cooper died, his karate instructor called out of the blue. He said he just wanted to tell me that he had been teaching karate for many years and had taught a lot of students during that time. He said, "But out of everyone, I just want to let you know he is the best student his age that I've ever had." He spent a full 30 minutes telling me what a remarkable and unique boy Cooper was.

I suppose an adult can fool people into thinking that he's considerate and kind, but a little boy can't. He was always helpful, always loving, and always kind – and when I say always, I mean *always*. Melanie said that every single week of his life, some stranger in Walmart would overhear his conversations with her, see how considerate and polite he was, and remark about what a special boy he was.

It wasn't just strangers. He was always friendly with the cashiers at Walmart. He would sit there and talk to them at the checkout aisle, and they would talk to him. He was genuinely interested in them, and they could tell.

That was the thing about Cooper. If you told him your pet's name and he saw you the next week, he would ask about your pet – by name. He would ask about your little girl or your momma. People would marvel, "Whoa! You remembered that? You're just four years old!"

None of us knew that it would all come to such an abrupt end. I guess the words, "It's time," can mean so many things. On February 24, 2004, they brought us great joy. On July 17, 2009, they brought us great sorrow.

Of course, we didn't know our little boy's time had come. We would have chosen a full lifetime here on earth for Cooper, complete with all the things parents want for their children. While my little boy lay still in my arms on that fateful day, his life slipping away, I pleaded with God to take me instead – to make it *my* time and not Cooper's.

But the Lord had decreed something different. Although I could not hear the words spoken, God had said, "It's time."

Five years after we received with open arms our beautiful gift from God, Samuel Cooper Jasper, we had to extend our arms and release him back to our Savior.

Cooper left this world in the same way he began: A police escort guided the funeral procession from the church to the cemetery as we would say goodbye to our only son.

Five years might not seem like a long life – and it isn't – but it was a life lived well. It was a life that impacted so many people. At his funeral, as Melanie and I and our girls were greeting people, I looked down the aisle of the church where nearly a thousand people gathered, and I saw these ten ladies coming towards us. I told Melanie, "I don't recognize them. Do you know who they are?" I wanted to know if I should remember their names.

Melanie said softly, "Those are our precious ladies from Walmart. The cashiers we went to each week."

After visitation was over and everyone had left the church, we saw a lone man sitting in the very back, hunched over and weeping. It was Cooper's karate instructor. The strongest man we knew could not leave because he was so broken.

The morning of the funeral, Paul, the barber came to our house, riding up on a motorcycle. We lived in a remote place, and Paul had never been to our home and only knew which county we lived in. So this tough, rugged guy simply rode around, stopping first at one farm, then another, asking if people knew where we lived. And he finally found us, rumbled up our gravel drive, and after coming inside, fell in our arms and wept on our shoulders.

How does a little boy have that kind of impact on so many people? It wasn't that we are a good family or that Melanie and I are great parents. There was just something special about Cooper and how he lived his life. Steve Hallman, a friend of ours, said Cooper's was a life lived well. Steve said when a person is born, he or she doesn't know if they have five years or fifty years or the next five minutes. But Cooper absolutely lived his life full bore and wide open, and he affected all these people in such a positive way.

Of course, I think it even goes deeper than that. I think Cooper impacted all these people because he was a living example of the gospel. He was so loving and he was so kind that I think God simply reached people through him. They might not even have realized it was God's love, but it touched them. People were genuinely touched by his life.

This is the thing about losing Cooper: If God had come to us in the beginning and said, "I'm going to give you a little boy, but it's a good news, bad news kind of thing. You will only have this boy for five years, and then there will be this terrible tragedy. You won't ever get to hold him again in this life. Do you still want him?"

Knowing the kind of boy that he was, we would still say yes. Of course, we miss him terribly every day; we would give anything to hear his laughter again or watch him run and play with his sisters while dressed as a super hero, something he enjoyed immensely. How we wish we could cuddle with him one more time or listen to him plan one more family trip. The pain of our loss is still enormous, but we wouldn't trade the blessing of knowing, loving, and being loved by Cooper, even for those five short years.

I don't think his karate teacher or the barber or the cashiers at Walmart or his classmates or countless other people would, either.

"For I know the plans I have for you," declares the Lord,
"plans to prosper you and not to harm you,
plans to give you hope and a future."

JEREMIAH 29:11

6

Before the Accident

After someone you love dies, you think about them all the time. You think about every detail of their life, especially details leading up to the day they died. You freeze frame the last conversation you had, the last meal, the last smile or wave. You carefully remember what they were wearing the last time you saw them and other tiny details. The weeks and months after the funeral you dwell on – no, you obsess over the memories you have. A movie plays in your mind's eye, and you can't seem to turn it off. Some of this is therapeutic; much of it is painful.

Like most people who have suffered a loss, we thought about the last few weeks of our son Cooper's life. We are an active, outdoors family and have never been accused of letting grass grow under our feet. We typically go wide open, staying busy and usually trying to pack too much into a day or weekend. Remembering the exciting full life young Cooper lived had us reflecting on the last couple of weeks of his life on earth. A few weeks prior, we had celebrated July 4th complete with a spectacular fireworks display. Also, Cooper and I went to the airport and went flying! Maddie had a birthday party with a luau theme at our cabin on the lake, and we captured it all on video. It was a perfect day filled with laughter, family, friends, cake, ice cream, and presents! Maddie had so much fun with her friends on her special day. Watching Cooper take his turn blindfolded swinging wildly at the pinata was hilarious. Later, as the birthday party migrated down to the lake for the kids to swim, Cooper entertained us by running full speed, jumping off the dock spread eagle and doing belly flops … on purpose! Our family is never bored, for sure. The weeks and days leading up to that terrible day were filled with action, adventure and so much fun.

I mentioned Cooper and me getting to fly! Allow me to tell you about the wonderful flight we took just days before Cooper's death. He and I went to our local airport, and I rented a Cessna 152 on a beautiful afternoon to do some local flying and enjoy some quality father and son time. I had tried to take him flying each year on his birthday and occasional other times, as often as money and weather would permit. I was hoping to get the smell of av-gas in his system at a young age and hopefully pass on my love for aviation to my only son.

After a thorough pre-flight, we settled into the cockpit, put on our headphones, contacted the tower and taxied for departure. As I looked over at my blonde-haired passenger the excitement and anticipation on his face captured the essence of the joy of flying. Cooper obviously didn't realize the "push to talk" feature. There is a push button on the steering wheel (yoke) of many airplanes that allows me to talk intermittently to either the air traffic controller in the control tower, my passengers or both. The passenger never knows when the button is pushed in. Cooper naturally assumed everyone was hearing all the conversations.

I took advantage of this hoping to build confidence in my young son. After getting the altimeter setting and necessary instructions from the tower, I released the mic button and pretended to continue talking to the tower. I told the controller that he needed to know that I was not alone at the controls. I proceeded to tell him in this mock conversation that my son, Cooper, was helping me fly and not to worry because even though he was only five years old, he was smart and a big helper to Momma and me and we're very proud of him. I continued to mention many of his great qualities and explained that we would be going very high and very fast, but Cooper wasn't scared because he was a brave, big boy. I continued "telling" the tower that this airplane was in the hands of not one but two pilots, and that Cooper was very capable. I laid it on thick in language a five-year-old could easily understand to boost his self esteem and reinforce how much we loved and cared for him.

As I glanced at Cooper from the corner of my eye during this conversation, it was rewarding to notice him sit up a little taller, grip the yoke tighter, with a focused serious look on his little face and his chest puffed out a bit. He had a look on his face that would've made Barney Fife proud! Always looking to affirm our children in as many ways as possible, I was grateful for how this teaching moment played out. After the pep talk, with taxi and run up complete, I then pressed the mic button and announced that we were ready for departure. As if on cue the ATC declared we were "cleared for take off," and if you didn't know any better, you would assume by the confident, professional tone of his voice that he had heard the whole conversation and was confirming it. As we applied full throttle and raced down the runway, Cooper was absolutely thrilled!

The record in my log book shows that the flight that day lasted one hour. My memory records it as one of the best days of my life! A daddy and his boy flying an airplane! Anyone who loves to fly can attest to what an incredible opportunity it is to share our passion with those we love. What an amazing adventure – second to none for making memories. We pilots often remember every detail of a flight because so much emotion, adrenaline, and planning are involved. The flight with my sweet son, Cooper, on July 8, 2009, is one I will remember as long as I live. It was only nine days later he died. I wouldn't trade anything for that incredibly special time not only to be with my little boy, but also to remind him that he was loved and cared for. Obviously, I had no clue that it would be our last flight together.

Five years doesn't seem like a long time, but we managed to have a schedule that included lots of time for church, school, family, and friends. Our girls were taking gymnastics lessons, drum and piano lessons, and participating in AWANA at church. Lauren and Cooper took karate lessons. They all played on a softball or tee ball team. We rode horses, fished, planted gardens; we did it all. We milked the most out of every holiday.

As we reflected on Cooper's last days here on earth, we were thankful that his days were full of love and life. Looking back we realized that in the last few weeks of his young life Cooper had gone flying, shot fireworks, gone swimming, ridden the wave runner, gone tubing for the first time, and enjoyed his sister's birthday party. He was riding his bike, swinging on the swing set, and riding a dune buggy on his last day. I'll try and share this next memory with you that's very personal and very difficult to tell.

Cooper was sitting on my lap, and he and I were mowing the lawn on the riding lawn mower just before the accident. As we were mowing, I was just taking everything in. The beautiful weather, our picturesque farm with gentle rolling hills and cows grazing. I was thoroughly enjoying our father and son time and was actually thinking about how sweet and special Cooper was (he was nearly a perfect child). I remember leaning down and over the roar of the mower, I put my lips to his ear and said, "Coop, Daddy is so proud of you. I love you so much and you make Momma and me so happy. You are such a good boy. You are strong and you're a good worker. Most of all I'm so glad you love Jesus. I'm so proud that you're my son, and I love you so much." Cooper laid his little cheek against my arm and gave me the biggest hug. Little did I know in only a few hours he would be gone from our arms and forever gone from this earth. As emotional as this memory is, I am so very thankful to God that He allowed me to have that special moment with my little boy. I'm forever grateful to the Lord, that Cooper's last few hours on earth weren't marked by getting scolded or any number of scenarios that could have brought enough heartache and guilt for a lifetime. Instead, our very last conversation was me telling him how proud I was of him and how much I loved him. Those last tender moments with Cooper were absolutely a gift from God and a wonderful treasured memory for which I will be eternally grateful.

It's a great comfort to know our son was encouraged and given words of affirmation. He was loved, and he was laughing and enjoying an adventure filled life right up to the very second he breathed his last breath.

Have mercy on me, O God, have mercy on me, for in you my soul takes refuge. I will take refuge in the shadow of your wings until the disaster has passed.

PSALM 57:1

7

The Accident

When we lived in town, Melanie and I longed to live in the country. We dreamed of going to sleep to the chirp of crickets and waking to the soothing sound of cows out in the pasture. Not much compares to sitting on a porch swing enjoying the night air and listening to a peaceful chorus of frogs down by the lake while your children laugh, play and run free in a wide open space. When you're several miles from the city's bright lights, you can stare into the night sky and easily pick out the North Star, the Big Dipper and the Milky Way.

We wanted to teach our children how to raise a garden, care for pets and livestock, and catch, clean, and cook a mess of fish. Call me old fashioned but I even enjoy the crunching sound your tires make when you turn off the paved road onto your own gravel drive.

We felt pioneer urgings to own some land, improve it and settle a home place. There is a certain satisfaction about owning land, since they aren't making any more of it. Also, folks in the country are just by nature neighborly. Nearly everything about country living appealed to us.

We realized our dream, got an amazing deal, and bought a small farm for the cost of an average home on a lot in the city. For us it was paradise – 28 acres fenced, a stocked lake, and horses, cows and an old Ford tractor. Our little world was nearly perfect. We attended a great church, had wonderful friends, and were happily married with four healthy children.

On the farm we thought about getting a four-wheeler. I protested, thinking it wouldn't be safe enough. I worried about it being so heavy and possibly flipping over backward. Then the kids suggested a golf cart – just to putter around the pasture and ferry supplies around the place. It seemed too top heavy, and Melanie and I said no.

We found a small dune buggy that was very low profile, only inches from the ground – almost an oversized go-cart. It had a full roll cage – roll bars on top and padded side roll bars. The dealer said it was practically impossible to flip over. Sure enough, with its wide stance it would only turn a short radius. (It seemed it took a half acre just to turn it around!) After buying it I was concerned about the powerful motor, so with help from my friend Clay, we adjusted the throttle to put a governor on it and allow it to only run at half speed. It was safe, it was fun; the kids loved it and rode it around the farm for a year without incident. (If you don't count the time my mother-in-law was driving with one of our girls and they drove straight through the most manure infested section of the pasture. It was hysterical and I'm pinching my nose right now just thinking about it.)

Cooper and I had been mowing when suddenly the riding lawn mower quit. We were unsuccessful trying to restart it. Melanie had gone to town to get a spark plug for the push-mower. Coop and I played for a while on the swing set, and then he rode his bicycle around in circles in the garage. I suggested we ride the dune buggy.

We prepared to ride up and down the dirt road in our pasture. As Cooper was buckling up, I said it wouldn't be necessary to wear a seat belt since we were here on the farm. He insisted and explained, "Dad, it's the right thing to do." My little man, always thorough, always conscientious, never did anything half way … ever. I was always amazed at how much I learned from him and how convicting it was to be around him sometimes. Cooper had an uncanny commitment to excellence even at such a young age.

We raced up and down the dirt lane in our pasture and played a game where I would slow down to a crawl, he would yell, "Flame on!" and I would floor it. "Flame on!" was an expression of his from a favorite super hero. It was his way of saying, "Go faster!"

With the wind in our hair we were belly laughing and having a blast. A father and a son. A daddy and his boy. After we rode for a short while, I thought I should head back to the house to check on our girls. I decided to turn the wheel, floor it, and do what we always called a "donut." It's where you spin the back end of a vehicle and then continue on straight. I turned the wheel, floored the accelerator and the back end started to spin around.

But then something went terribly wrong. The dune buggy flipped over. I was not buckled in, so the rollover threw me out, but I was unhurt. Immediately I glanced over at the dune buggy lying on its side. Cooper remained securely fastened in his seat belt. While there was not a scratch on him, his eyes were fixed straight ahead. I ran to him and tried to talk to him, but got no response. There was a tiny trickle of blood coming from one nostril. Panic grabbed me. I began to pray. After unbuckling Cooper, I laid him on the ground. I was doing CPR on my five-year-old son looking into his lifeless eyes and begging God to please spare his life and take mine instead. I continued pleading with God, even while my mind was denying that this was happening.

I put him over my shoulder and started running to the house, which was several hundred yards away. Afraid the run was jostling him too much, I would stop, lay him on the ground and do CPR again. His breathing was shallow and while he was on his back it sounded like he was drowning. Not knowing what else to do, I put Cooper over my shoulder and continued to run the rest of the way home. The whole time I was running, I was pleading with the Lord, "Please God, save my son! Please heal him, Lord! Oh, Lord! Oh, God, please!" I was praying over and over, "I need a miracle."

I arrived at the house, banged on the door and when the girls answered,

I quickly explained what had happened and how serious it was and told them to please hurry and get the phone. I immediately called 911 and requested a helicopter. I was informed it was en route to another emergency and was unavailable. I tried to give our address but in my panic I couldn't remember our address or the name of the church on the main road in front of our house or our neighbor's farm to use as a reference point.

I called Mel, explained how dire the situation was and asked her to call 911 and give them our address. Due to the quick call and the limited information I gave Mel, she assumed it was an accident involving the riding lawnmower. In between calls I continued to give Cooper CPR. The girls prayed like adult saints of God. Sadie and Maddie were obviously very shaken but instead of falling apart, they immediately started praying fervently and out loud. I remember Maddie turned away from us and looked heavenward with both arms raised and prayed, "Lord God, You see what's happening here! This is my brother. Lord, we need Your help right now. Jesus, please, we know You can heal him. We know You're able to do this. Please God, raise him up!" It's odd how you can be panic stricken and impressed by something in the same moment, but I remember how inspiring it was to see this little six-year-old demonstrate such mature faith beyond her years and pray like the saints of old.

Melanie tells the story of similar response when, a year earlier, I lay dying in our pasture after a near fatal horseback riding accident. Melanie said she shouted for the children to pray while she ran to my side and they all lined up, kneeling at our white wooden fence with their eyes closed and their hands folded, boldly praying that God would spare their daddy's life! As Christian parents it does our hearts good to know that when calamity suddenly strikes, our children intuitively knew what to do and who to turn to even at such a young age. I couldn't have been more proud of Sadie and Maddie than in that horrible, horrible moment.

I'm not sure how much time passed, but a patrol car came up the driveway, and the deputy took my place attending to Cooper. Then the ambulance came and EMTs took over. Then Melanie arrived and collapsed as soon as she got out of the car. She's the strongest woman I know; I've never seen her ever flinch at anything. She had our children by natural childbirth, played softball, and is very athletic. She is gorgeous and girly when she needs to be and a tough farm girl when it's required. To see her buckle and fall to the ground was heartwrenching. The sheriff, who by now was on the scene, told us to ride with him to the hospital. Of course we wanted to be with our baby in the ambulance, but he insisted we allow the EMTs to do their jobs.

I apologized to Mel all the way to the hospital. She kept reassuring me it was an accident and there was nothing to apologize for. We prayed the entire way to the hospital, hoping for a miracle but deep down I sensed Cooper had died in my arms. We followed them into the emergency room and watched the doctor and nurses feverishly work on him for several minutes. Then we watched as the medical team suddenly stopped, the doctor looked up at the clock and called the time of his death. It resembled a scene from a movie, but I knew it wasn't. This was really happening. Our son had died.

Standing with us in a corner of the emergency room, only several feet from where they had been working on Cooper, were our dear friends Rev. Robert Garland and his wife Lora and Neel Dean. Melanie's brother, Zach, and our neighbor, James Harold Keith, were there also. Other close friends had gathered just outside the emergency room door. The doctor walked over a few steps, very professional and compassionate and said something like, "We're so sorry, we did everything we could." The only way I knew to respond to him was with Scripture: "The Lord giveth and the Lord taketh away, Blessed be the name of the Lord."

When we stepped into the hallway, we were greeted by our pastor, family and friends. Sounds seemed muffled and everything seemed to be happening in slow motion. It was almost eerie, like I was having an out of body experience. I spotted Bro. Don Wildmon down the long hallway. He was steadying himself, holding the wall with one hand, with his other hand over his mouth. He was wailing, not just crying. In that moment I was impacted by the sight of this reserved and respected Christian leader so moved and broken by the loss of this little boy. But Bro. Don and Cooper had a special relationship. Melanie told me that whenever they would visit AFA, as soon as they entered the building, Cooper would ask with great excitement, "Can I go see him?" The "him" was Don Wildmon. Cooper always wanted to pop in on Bro. Don before he made his way to my office. Melanie was sensitive to how busy Bro. Don was, but he always made time for Cooper. The two had little games they would play, including giving high fives and Don throwing Cooper up in the air. For all of Don Wildmon's focused and firm demeanor, he really has a soft spot for children and the little ones respond well to him, too. Without a doubt, Don Wildmon was one of Cooper's heroes and Cooper was Bro. Don's little buddy.

The hospital staff secured a little room for Melanie and me and brought Cooper in. They encouraged us to take our time before they took him away to the morgue. Take him away to the morgue. Every fiber in me was rejecting the words we were hearing. Those words seemed so bizarre. He's only a little boy, our little boy. So full of life. No one laughs and loves and thinks and lives like this little fellow. How could this be possible? Surely this is a terrible, scary nightmare and we're going to wake up and everything is going to be all right. We were playing together just minutes ago. He can't be dead. He can't be! That's not the right answer. Everything in us seemed to be screaming, *Please, no, no, no, no!*

Melanie and I sat stunned alone in the room. Eventually, the cold, bare room seemed like some sort of holy ground. Just the two of us who brought this beautiful baby into the world were now faced with the unbelievable task of having to somehow tell him goodbye. We ran our fingers through his hair and just sat there, dazed. Maybe we were in shock. It was our beautiful Cooper – except he was not breathing or talking. They were his little hands, his little feet. It was his handsome face, but his brilliant blue eyes were just staring. He was not responding to us as we told him how much we loved him. Time stood still. Even as we were clinging to our faith in God, it was without a doubt the most crushing, desperate, helpless, lowest point of our lives. I really can't tell you how long we stayed there or how we even managed to say goodbye. Or how we managed to get up and walk out that door. I don't remember any of those details.

The next thing I do remember, however, is Tim and Alison Wildmon's kindness and compassion. They helped us into their van and took us by Melanie's brother's home to pick the girls up and then they drove us home. I have no memory of the drive to our house. Two of our dearest friends, Greg Johnson and Clay Cruse, were there. Our Sunday school teacher, Chris Barker, and long time friend and co-worker, Buster Wilson, and a few others were waiting for us as well. For Mel and me, both of our families lived 300 miles away, and they were immediately en route. Buster, who along with being a co-worker is also a pastor, offered wise words of comfort. He knew that I would obviously be dealing with guilt and told Melanie and me, "Scripture teaches that there is an appointed time for each person to die. You could have carried that sweet baby around all day on a feather pillow and something else would have happened today. Please don't blame yourself." The timing for that counsel was perfect and the words helped more than he realized.

We sat in the living room and cried and just tried to process everything through the shock and denial. We were in a stupor. Our sweet friends prayed for us, and it just meant so much that they were there. Everyone was so gracious, so full of love and compassion. Nearly everyone eventually left. Greg and Clay refused to go. Amazing those two. I was very stern and all but ordered them to leave, imagining how much anguish and tears and hysteria would follow. But Greg and Clay responded with equal stubbornness. They said they were not leaving under any circumstances. They stayed up all night. What amazing friends. Absolutely amazing! Little did we know how desperately we would need them the next morning. We were totally out of it. You really need capable, loving friends and family around you in that kind of melt-down mode.

Alone in our room and exhausted, we were trying to wrap our brains around everything that had happened in just a matter of hours. In our state of semi-shock, the lines were blurred between what was real and what wasn't. We weren't able to fully grasp the reality of it all, but this much was undeniable: We knew our lives would never be the same.

Surely He hath borne our griefs, and carried our sorrows:
yet we did esteem Him stricken, smitten of God,
and afflicted.

ISAIAH 53:4 (KJV)

8

After the Accident

Immediately after I opened my eyes the next morning I was filled with a sense of relief. It was just a nightmare. *I've been dreaming, and everything will be back to normal now that I'm awake,* I thought. But it only took seconds for the truth to jolt me back to reality regarding what had happened the day before. Melanie and I held each other and sobbed uncontrollably for a long time, and then we got it together enough to go downstairs.

Greg and Clay stayed up all night talking in our living room and praying for us. They were an absolute Godsend. They'd made breakfast for our daughters and were keeping them entertained for us. After a very emotional morning, Greg called the funeral home and made an appointment for us later in the day. Out-of-town family members were starting to trickle in.

There was a knock on the door and a man stood there, someone we barely knew and who had never been to our home before. He asked to come in. He stood before me and placed his hands squarely on my shoulders. He looked me in the eyes and proceeded to tell me his story. There was a fence completely surrounding the swimming pool at their home, but he had inadvertently left the gate unlatched, resulting in the drowning of his young son. He emphatically told me, "Your situation was an accident, and you can't blame yourself. You can't bring Cooper back or change anything or help anyone by punishing yourself." Because he had "been there," this man had earned the right to be heard, and he delivered a powerful word of ministry at just the right time. I'm grateful for Mr. Boutot's boldness. He gave of his time, went out of his way, and took a risk that his message might not be received well. It was later that day or the next that a man with a similar story stopped by to offer nearly the same advice. This man gave permission for his daughter to go horseback riding, and the results were fatal. He struggled with blaming himself. I don't remember the details of our conversation but I do recall how helpful it was to hear at such a crucial time.

Greg and I walked down our gravel drive. Greg's first-born son, Miles, had died of leukemia when he was just three years old. Over the years, I'd asked him about Miles' death and he had never been able to talk about it. As we walked Greg poured out his heart about his love for his son. He talked about the day he died and offered me some much-needed practical, loving counsel. Later Clay and I walked and talked as well, and he also shared some much needed Biblical wisdom coupled with genuine compassion and concern. The love I felt and the strength I gleaned from those two men early in my grief journey was priceless.

It was time to go to the funeral home to make arrangements. On our way to the funeral home we had the radio tuned to American Family Radio. I remember hanging on to each word, allowing each hope-filled phrase to fill my heart. I thank God for Christian music and for Christian radio stations. That day the lyrics were a lifeline to us and buoyed us as we stumbled forward.

After we arrived at the funeral home, we had a meeting to plan the funeral arrangements. We were thankful that those around the table in the meeting were dear close friends and providentially half of the small number had actually experienced the death of a child. Who better to help us navigate through this? Greg and Frances Johnson, as I mentioned earlier, had lost their son, Miles. Two of our dearest friends, Durick and Debbie Hayden, were there, and they had suffered through the death of their middle son, Chris, only three years earlier. Melanie's mom, Kandi, had just arrived in town and joined us near the end of the appointment. She had lost her husband, Melanie's father. There are many footprints on this path of grieving. It was a blessing to have this team of trusted friends who had done this before to help coach us and lovingly guide us.

Our dear friend Randall Murphree was there. We wrote the obituary with his assistance. I then made a call to my radio co-host, Eric Faulds, and asked if he would create a slide show using some of our pictures of Cooper. Because Eric is a perfectionist and very professional, we were completely confident it would be done right. And it was. Then the funeral director led us into another room where we were instructed, "Pick out a casket for your little boy." Those words were among the most abstract I've ever heard uttered. The words seemed profoundly out of place. "Pick out a casket for Cooper." All the words we heard were surreal. It was like being on the outside looking in to try to describe the emotions we were experiencing. To put it in perspective, just the evening before, our world was perfect and I was playing with my only son. A daddy and his little boy making memories. Here we were mid morning the following day at the funeral home being asked, "Which casket do you want for your son?" God help us!

Caskets shouldn't be that small, I thought as we were shown different selections. There were many other painful, random thoughts ricocheting in my mind. Parents aren't supposed to outlive their children. This is unnatural and completely out of order. Picking out a casket for your child is the most wretched, horrible, rotten experience for any parent to endure. May God spare you from ever having to experience that searing hot poker to your soul.

After we left the funeral home, to add insult to injury, we made our way across town where another heart-wrenching decision needed to be made – selecting a grave site in the cemetery. It's interesting how you go through your life convinced you're getting instruction on everything you need to know from A to Z, and yet here we were struggling with decisions that had never even crossed our minds. Now they couldn't be escaped. We had to decide.

After returning home our house resembled some kind of campaign headquarters or a staging area of sorts. Our friend, Kathy Coats, a co-worker and long-time church member had taken over our kitchen and was doling out duties to eager volunteer food helpers. People were pouring in with covered dishes in hand. This may be true of other parts of the country, but one of the many things I love about the South is how any time there is an illness or death, bringing food is a common expression of love and sympathy.

Close friends were busy on their phones giving directions to the many out-of-town family and friends who were coming. Some were parking cars. Bro. Don had positioned himself as a sentry to stand guard at our gate, carding people to see if they were immediate family members. If not, he was instructing them to please come back after a few days. Others were setting up many card tables in our living room and den. There were so many people and such a flurry of activity. Friends had cleaned, and so many had brought food that we were unaware of. Over the next few days and weeks there were so many acts of kindness that we didn't even find out about until we were told much later. How humbling to experience that much love. It was amazing to have such a strong network of family and friends. I realize that's not the case in everyone's situation. Melanie and I thought about how heartbreaking it must be for a person living far from home in a new town, living among strangers with no close friends, family or church members, to experience a death like we did. It didn't seem fair for us to have all of this help and all of this prayer when others may not. We were blessed, and it was humbling. I can't imagine getting through a tragedy without lots of support.

With our home resembling some sort of base camp and seeing so many close friends that we hadn't seen in years, I remember briefly thinking how it almost seemed like a family reunion or a wedding was about to take place. But the opposite was true. Our sadness and pain would quickly multiply beyond anything we could imagine. With family, friends, and prayer in such abundance, however, God used it to keep us going.

And we know that all things work together for good to them that love God, to them who are the called according to His purpose.

ROMANS 8:28 (KJV)

9

Flipped

I asked our oldest daughter, Lauren, to share from a sister's heart. This is her story.

February 24, 2004. Thinking back I can almost smell the sterile hospital air of North Mississippi Medical Center's Women's Hospital. I can almost feel the coldness of the wooden door pressed against my eight-year-old ear as I strained to hear what was going on just beyond it. Being the oldest of three girls at the time, I had the assigned role of professional hospital-door-sitter-out-in-fronter, complete with the official "I'm the Big Sister" outfit. I guess somehow I assumed this day would be like the others when Jaspers were added to our family: I would walk in and find the usual – another blonde-haired, blue-eyed baby girl.

Finally, the door opened and revealed the excitement that had been going on out of sight. It was a sight I will not soon forget: the tiniest little boy, wrapped in some space age yellow paper and foil, hands folded. I remember immediately wanting to change the baby's diaper before I could confidently call him a him. But even more than that, I had never felt so much love for something that looked so much like a potato. His eyes had that jelly stuff on them, but I was sure they were blue. Staring at this just seconds-old, wrinkly little creature, I knew someone special had just been born, and little did I know, a best friend.

His name was Samuel Cooper, and I was hooked.

I was only five and six years old when my sisters were born, so I have a much less vivid memory of their earliest days. But of course, being the mature and sophisticated second-grader that I was now, I had a much better understanding of what was going on in Cooper's life. Not that much was going on, other than smelling quite frequently and putting Old Faithful to shame. If there was a baby Olympics, the kid was a shoe-in for a gold medal in going through diapers. Literally. He was squishy too, so that was cool.

Fast-forward. For whatever reasons, my parents, mainly my dad, after 40 some odd years of life, decided he was a farmer. Naturally, we did what all normal people do and bought a farm. To the outside world this may have seemed more than a tad off-the-wall, but for us, it was just another day in life with J.J. Jasper.

The story behind my chapter, though, begins in July of 2009. My mom, sisters, Cooper and I were meeting my aunt and grandmother at Cracker Barrel in Meridian, Mississippi, to drop me off for my annual visit to the state's coast. I remember this day as if it were yesterday. The day was sunny and 75 degrees, with a little breeze in the air. It was lunchtime, but of course I ordered breakfast – my favorite Cracker Barrel meal – and of course a certain towheaded little boy sat right beside me. As usual he was accompanied by his Batman action figure.

As brunch came to an end, and we were just about to go our separate ways, I remember a little hand tugging at my shirt with urgency. "Lala," Coop said, using his favorite nickname for me, "take this to remember me." He handed me a small Spiderman flip-book filled with Cooper-drawn pictures of every superhero – ever. I reminded him I was just going to be gone for a week. "Please," he insisted. "Take this to remember me."

I thought, *Remember you? Okay little dude, whatever you say.*

In retrospect, this typical family outing on a typical summer day will forever be some of my sweetest, most cherished memories. You see, on this day, I saw my best friend for the last time.

On this particular trip I would be attending my first-ever church camp as a high schooler, which in the world of youth groups is kind of a coming-of-age thing. My aunt and uncle, Kasie and Jeremy Ulmer, had been the youth pastors of a church in Biloxi, Mississippi, for some time and had invited me to go with their group. The camp was called "Student Life @ the Beach." The sense of anticipation was so strong because it was a week with some of my best friends, the beach, and Jesus. I didn't think life could get any better. Finally the day to leave for the coast came, the vans were loaded, and we were off!

The theme of this year's camp was "Flip" – Our lives can be flipped upside down with one phone call. Tragedy will strike. It's not if, but when. The speaker for the entire week, Matt Chandler, urged this message over and over again. "All it takes is one phone call," he would say, "and your life can be flipped." For a week our hearts were being prepared and readied to be able to give Christ the glory when we encounter the trials of this world.

But it was almost as if this message had been placed on Matt's heart just for my ears. I couldn't escape that feeling, and I just couldn't get enough. I've never felt so much like a sponge in my life. At the same time, however, the teenager in me felt as invincible as ever.

On the morning of Friday, July 17, I was on the mountaintop. That evening was the last worship session of camp. I was so sad for this sweet experience to be over but so excited about Jesus and life. My little heart was so full I could barely stand it.

Little did I know the phone had just rung.

As worship was just about to begin, I felt a hand grab me out of my aisle seat. My eyes locked with two bloodshot blue eyes. Kasie's mouth was moving but my ears just couldn't keep up. There had been an accident. It was Cooper. It involved the family dune buggy and he was being rushed to the emergency room and we had to go – now.

Please understand, in the Jasper household someone breaking an arm or getting thrown off of a horse was nothing new. But, even then I knew. Something was different. I packed my things as if nothing were wrong, more than anything just trying to convince myself. I remember walking into a room full of big weeping men and their heavy-hearted wives and my uncle – my sweet Uncle Jeremy – in a very broken sentence telling me my dad was on the phone, and he needed to talk to me. Everything inside of me screamed, *RUN!* I already knew; I just didn't want to hear it; because if I heard it, it became real, and reality was exactly the place I did not want to be.

"Lauren, I'm going to need you to hold on to everything you've learned this week.

"No, Dad, wait! Please stop, don't say it!

"Cooper isn't with us anymore."

Selfishly, as I fell to the floor, I couldn't help but think of the outside world with carefree toes in the sand, while just beyond sliding glass doors a family's world was crumbling under their feet. Every hair, every pore, every breath that left my lungs, ached for just one more look at that contagious smile. One more, "I love you, Lala." One more anything.

Being a newly teenaged girl, emotions running rampant was just part of life, but for the next few weeks I was numb, completely void of any emotion. The tears, though, seemed to come almost involuntarily. The steady trickle of people in and out of our home was like morphine for the soul, but one day without warning it all stopped.

And then there were five. What now? We were a broken unit, a team lacking a player, but we had each other and that's all we knew. We also had the hope and promise of joy and new mercies in the morning to cling to – which we did, oh so tightly. Hand in hand, step by weak-kneed step we walked through the valley. We endured the darkest of nights.

But we also experienced what God promised: "When you pass through the waters, I will be with you; and through the rivers, they shall not overwhelm you; when you walk through fire you shall not be burned, and the flame shall not consume you" (Isaiah 43:2, ESV).

My flesh and my heart may fail, but God is the strength of my heart and my portion forever.

PSALM 73:26

10

Melanie's Chapter

Old Testament character Job had many trials and troubles but remained faithful to the Lord. More than one person has compared me to Job because I endured a near fatal horseback riding accident, followed the next year by the death of our only son.

The real Job in our family is my wife, Melanie. She is the strongest and most courageous woman I know. Melanie was a daddy's girl. Her father died March 14, 2008, at a young age after a short bout with cancer. Only days later she experienced a miscarriage on Easter Sunday morning. Later that same year on Labor Day, I had the horseback riding accident that caused me to be hospitalized for 49 days, and 7 of those days were in the intensive care unit. Throughout this ordeal, Melanie never left my side. She slept in the chair beside my hospital bed and worked around the clock coordinating with doctors and nurses, all the while keeping everything at home on schedule. I don't know how you moms get all your work done, but it makes me tired just watching my wife keeping those plates on sticks spinning and all of the juggling balls in the air!

To be in Melanie's shoes and looking through her eyes, here was the view in 2008. Let's see, her dad died, she had a miscarriage (it was actually her second in seven months) and her husband (that would be me) almost died. Can you imagine? When you would assume the worst was over the very next year, the summer of 2009 her only son died in the accident on our family farm. Yes, Melanie is the strongest woman I have ever known. She is my hero and it has been both inspiring and humbling to watch her endure so much without totally collapsing. Her faith in God has remained intact throughout these ordeals and she continues to trust the Lord and turn to Him to receive grace and mercy in her times of need.

Melanie is a Proverbs 31 woman. I know how I felt as a father losing my son, but I didn't carry Cooper nine months. And as much as I loved him and knew him, Melanie knew him better. She carried him, nursed him and taught him all of the early skills to move him from infant to toddler. I'm sometimes a little jealous that she spent more time with Cooper than any other person. But having said that, it seems that would greatly compound the pain and grief. I urged Melanie to write this chapter. After much prayer she agreed. I just asked her to share from her unique perspective as Cooper's mom. I encouraged her, "Just tell from a mother's heart anything you want to say or feel led to share."

She has earned the right to be heard. It is my great honor to introduce – Melanie's chapter.

I grew up in a Godly home with wonderful parents and an amazing brother and sister. God blessed me with the most incredible childhood any kid could ever ask for, and I wouldn't trade it or change a single day of it.

But I also went through the rebellious teenage years and made some life altering mistakes. However, God has been faithful to see me through some difficult life lessons and some really dark times, even a broken marriage and becoming a single parent to my sweet daughter Lauren when she was only an infant.

I grew up in church and I mean literally grew up there. We were there every time the doors were opened and sometimes when they weren't. Because of that Godly upbringing and a prayer prayed as a child with my momma, I thought I was a Christian, and I very well may have been.

But it wasn't until August 1997, at one of the lowest points of my life, that I surrendered my life one hundred percent to Jesus. He changed my life, I was a new creation. The old was gone and the new had come!

It was only a short time after I surrendered to Christ that I met and married my wonderful husband, J.J. He is the real deal. If you know him from the radio, what you hear on the radio is genuine; he loves Jesus with every fiber of his being, and God has truly blessed me with him!

God was making all of my dreams come true. He had given me a husband who adored both me and my two-year-old daughter, Lauren. Then He blessed us with three more precious children, Sadie, Maddie and Cooper. Three babies in 36 months - life was good – life was busy, but life was good! It was the fairytale life I had always wanted, but then fast forward to October 3, 2007. and that's when the fairytale began unraveling.

I had a very difficult miscarriage. Before my own miscarriage I never quite understood why women would go through depression after a losing a baby. I honestly thought there was no way they could possibly have been that connected to the baby they were carrying. I mean, they had never laid eyes on him, held her, or touched the sweet-soft skin, but boy was I wrong! Up to that point in my life, that was one of the most difficult things I have ever been through. The thought that I would never get to know that sweet baby this side of heaven was extremely hard to cope with. I now understand the sadness and depression that comes with the loss of an unborn child.

Not many months after my miscarriage when I finally felt normal again, my sweet daddy, whom I loved with my whole heart, was diagnosed with cancer and in just three-and-a-half weeks after his diagnosis, he went home to be with Jesus. My whole world seemed to be unraveling. Daddy was always such a big part of my life. He was one of those "larger than life" kind of people and anyone who didn't get to meet him really missed out.

Then as if that wasn't enough, one week to the day after my daddy's funeral, on Easter Sunday morning, I had a second miscarriage. Needless to say, my world was falling apart, but God carried us through. I clung to Psalm 34:18, "God is close to the brokenhearted." And let me just say, "Thank you, Jesus! That verse is true!"

Life seemed to be returning to normal, but then on Labor Day, 2008 just six months after Daddy passed away, J.J. was in a near fatal horseback riding accident and for seven days clung to life in the intensive care unit. He was in the hospital for 49 days, so I don't have to tell you wives and mothers how hard it was to watch my husband suffer while at the same time taking care of our children who were then thirteen, seven, six and four years old.

Our children, however, were very resilient through all of this. It is amazing how much joy children can bring to help cushion sadness. They truly are gifts from God! And they make life fun and interesting. Oh, to see life through the eyes of a child.

My girls – Lauren, Sadie, Maddie and now my little Kasie James – are simply amazing and there is so much I could tell you about each one of them, but right now I want to tell you about my little man, Cooper. We were on "cloud nine" when we found out we were having a boy. I had dreamed my whole life of having a little boy. I had always heard about the special bond between a momma and her son, and I saw it first hand with my own mother and brother.

When Cooper made his entrance into the world, he was a special blessing from the beginning. He had a gentle, loving spirit, beautiful blonde hair, blue eyes and a little dimple on his left cheek that was always present because he was always smiling. And he had a way of making everyone else around him smile. He truly cared for everyone; I can't think of one person that he didn't get along with, but his favorite people in the world were his sisters. I am and will be forever grateful for the love they had for each other. He loved life and played hard every day from sun up to sun down. He was all boy and loved being outside, though strangely he wasn't ever excited about getting dirty.

I prayed literally every single day of Cooper's life that God would turn this little man into a mighty man of valor, a mighty warrior, and use him for His glory. We diligently taught him that men were to be the head of the homes, that they needed to be wise and always seek the Lord. We taught him (and the girls for that matter) that a good strong hand-shake was a great asset and we would practice those handshakes often. J.J. had already begun teaching him how to work with tools and let him figure out how to do certain tasks on his own, such as tightening screws or hammering nails. It blessed my heart to watch him mimicking his daddy and becoming more and more like him all the time.

I was looking forward to the day when I could see that little blonde-haired, dimple-faced boy all grown up, big and strong and living boldly and unashamedly for the Lord. It was easy to picture that because I can honestly say he never gave us any trouble and loved to please us, but more than that he loved to please Jesus. He loved the Lord with his entire heart. It always amazed us how mature he was regarding the things of the Lord. We would half jokingly say he might be the next Billy Graham.

He loved the Lord so much that the Lord was constantly on his little mind even at only five years old. For example, one particular Sunday morning, we were leaving the sanctuary where the pastor had just delivered a great sermon on Jonah. Cooper walked outside heading to the car and was crying and very distraught. J.J. and I asked him what was wrong. He began crying louder, "I don't want to be like Jonah! I don't want to run from God! I want to do what He wants me to, but I don't know what that is! I don't know what He wants me to do!"

I think J.J. and I just stared at each other for a few seconds not believing what we were hearing from such a young child, and at the same time wondering how to calm him down. J.J. just bent down and got on his level and said something like, "Son, it's okay. You have a long time to figure out what God wants you to do for Him. I promise you, you will know when He tells you." Then he finished with, "Now let's go get something to eat." That seemed to suffice. He wiped his tears and we went to eat, but were still amazed at his deep desire to obey the Lord.

What an amazing child! Never ever did we think that his time here on the earth with us would be so short, but on July 17, 2009, a day I will never forget, Cooper was called home to be with Jesus. It was a beautiful, near perfect day, and one of the most fun days in my entire memory. You see, I was "stuck" at home because J.J.'s truck was in the shop, so he had taken my car to work. I was so frustrated; I didn't have time to be "stuck" at the house. I had things to do. We desperately needed groceries, and I had a few other pressing errands to run, but I am so grateful – eternally grateful – that it was just me and the kids "stranded" at the house all day long with no agenda, no pressure to be anywhere but right there at home. We had so much fun and made memories that I will always cherish.

We had planned for a quiet Friday evening at home. J.J. was going to mow the yard after work, and I was going to grab a few of those much needed groceries and then relax and settle in for a nice night of just being together. However, that is not what happened at all. I did go to Walmart to pick up the groceries and a spark plug J.J. had asked me to buy, but before leaving, I told him I wanted to take the kids with me so he could get the yard mowed without having to worry about them. But he insisted I go by myself because it was rare that I ever got to be alone. So, that's what I did. However, just as I was backing out of the driveway I had a strong, sudden desire to say good bye to J.J. and Cooper again, something I will regret not doing the rest of my life. It was such a nagging feeling that I actually pulled back up the driveway to get out to hug them but didn't because I thought to myself, *I'm being silly ... that's crazy. I'm going to be right back.*

So, off I went. And on the way there, I was listening to beautiful praise and worship music when my dear friend, Frances Johnson, came to my mind. I actually couldn't stop thinking about her. She had lost her son, Miles, to leukemia at only three years of age and I thought to myself, *I cannot imagine losing a child. I don't know how I would ever get over it.* Miles still comes up in conversation every time I am with Frances. She must still hurt every single day even though it's been 17 years since he passed away. I began to pray for Frances, and with tears streaming down my face, continued to pray out loud for her the entire way to Walmart. After regaining my composure, I went inside to shop not knowing that in 30 minutes I would be in the check-out aisle, aisle 11 to be exact, receiving the phone call that would change my life forever. I will never be able to go down that aisle again without memories of that dreadful call.

It was J.J. on the other end and in a panic he said, "Honey, there's been an accident, and I don't think Cooper is going to make it. I need you to call 911. I already called and talked to them but I can't remember our address and want to make sure they know where we are." I left my buggy and all of the contents with the cashier just staring at me and ran as fast as I could to my car, calling 911 as I ran. I just assumed that it was a lawn mowing accident, because when I left the house Cooper was riding on J.J.'s lap mowing with him. Once on the line with the dispatcher, I gave her the correct address and begged for a life flight to be sent because we lived so far from the hospital. She said, "We will try."

I then asked her if she could tell me what happened exactly. She was hesitant. I pleaded with her to tell me. I said, "I know my son is badly hurt and I am assuming something happened with the lawn mower." She then very calmly said, "It was an accident involving a dune buggy." I told the dispatcher thank you for telling me and then got off the phone.

A rush of emotions flooded over me: I cannot even begin to explain the agony I was in. I wanted to be there with Cooper right then, not driving in a car trying to get to him, and then I was struck with another horrible thought, *Oh, no! If it was the dune buggy, more than likely Sadie was driving, which was very common.* She loved to drive that dune buggy and was very good at it. And then I began to scream aloud, "Oh, Jesus, please be with Sadie because she will never be able to forgive herself if Cooper doesn't make it." And then all I could do while speeding down the road to our home was pray the only words that would come out, "JESUS, JESUS, JESUS!!!! Please Jesus, breathe life into my baby!" I screamed these words all the way home.

As I sped up the gravel drive I could see the lights of police cars and the ambulance. I had to park away from the house to leave room for the ambulance to get out. I hardly had the strength in my legs to get up the driveway. My entire body was racked with chills like the ones you get when you're so cold your jaw won't quit shivering. When I finally laid eyes on my sweet baby boy lying on the ground lifeless with the paramedics working on him, I knew – I just knew in my heart he was gone, and I collapsed to the ground as our neighbor helped catch me. I still was praying aloud, "Jesus, Jesus, Jesus! Please breathe life into my baby!" However, something inside was telling me to gather up my strength because he wasn't going to make it.

While I was still on the ground next to Cooper, J.J. came over and he was crying, saying, "I'm so sorry!" over and over again. It was only then that I realized that it wasn't Sadie driving. I hugged J.J. – I think, it really is all a blur – but I do remember leaving Cooper while they were still working on him, and both J.J. and I went over to love on our precious girls who were with a deputy and another one of our neighbors. All I could do is hug them and say, "It's going to be okay. We are going to get through this. Just keep praying for Cooper." And then J.J. and I went back to be with him.

They put Cooper in the ambulance, and the sheriff, Neal Davis, who could sense that we wanted to ride in the ambulance, said, "Y'all should ride with me. They need to focus on working on him." So we agreed and got in the back of his car. He was such a kind man. All of the law enforcement and medical personnel on the scene were wonderful.

The ride to the hospital was very strange to say the least. Just knowing that my baby was in the ambulance in front of me and I couldn't do anything to help him but pray was a very surreal feeling. I remember lying over, burying my head in J.J.'s chest and the two of us just crying and him going over everything that happened and then begging me to forgive him. I tried to tell him I wasn't angry with him, that I knew he was only having fun with his son, but I know his mind was spinning and he was just trying to figure out how he could turn back time and change things.

I remember asking the sheriff, "Do you think he is going to make it? Do you think he is already gone? Is it too late to pray?"

He answered, "It's never too late." I knew that, but my mind was all over the place; in fact, there really aren't words to explain how or what I was feeling.

When we arrived at the hospital, we jumped out of the car to be with Cooper. We could tell by the way the doctor and nurses were working on him that the outcome wasn't going to be good. There in a little side room with us were a few dear friends and my wonderful brother, Zach. J.J. and I just held each other and wept, and just then a terrible fear came over me. Reality was setting in that I was losing my son, and that more than likely it would change my husband forever. I looked at J.J. and I begged him, "Please don't let this change you. It was an accident. You were only having fun with him, that's what daddies do with their sons. I want you to still be that fun man I fell in love with. Please! Please don't let this change you!" I don't remember what he said to me, but I could tell he was listening and taking it in. Then our attention switched back to worrying about Cooper.

It wasn't long – maybe just five or ten minutes – after Cooper was brought in that they told us how sorry they were and that they had done everything humanly possible but couldn't save him. I can't describe what I felt in that moment, but I recall what my brave husband did. He went over to Cooper's bedside and quoted the words of Job, "The Lord giveth and the Lord taketh away, blessed be the name of the Lord." I knew right then and there that we were going to make it – it would be excruciatingly difficult, but we were going to make it.

They allowed us to say our final goodbyes. There he was, my gorgeous little boy with not even a scratch on him, now lifeless. How can someone be so alive one minute and gone from this life the next? It was hard to even imagine leaving the hospital without him, much less walking into our Cooperless home. I laid my head beside his and ran my fingers through his soft blonde hair. And kissed his sweet cheeks and his little hands, and for one last time I kissed those precious little feet of his. He always loved for me to kiss his feet for some reason, we even made a game out of it. The pain of peeling myself away from him was almost unbearable. I didn't want to leave him there in that cold room. It didn't seem right. I couldn't process the realness of it all. I wanted it all to be an awful nightmare, but it wasn't. I pulled myself together because there were many outside in the hall waiting to love on us. I remember seeing everyone and thinking again, *This just can't be happening.*

While still at the hospital, trying to wrap our minds around all of this – which is impossible to do in the first hours or even days – we knew we had to tell our oldest daughter Lauren about the accident. She was away at Student Life Camp with my sister, Kasie, and brother-in-law, Jeremy. I asked J.J. if he would make the call. I didn't think I could do it. I had no idea what I would say. He picked up his phone and proceeded to make the painful call, and I remember the wise words he started the conversation with. He said, "Hey Lauren, this is Daddy, and I've got something to tell you. Something very bad has happened, but before I tell you, I want you to hold on to everything you know about God and all you have learned this week at camp." He paused for a second and then continued, "Cooper was in an accident, and he is no longer with us. He didn't make it." I couldn't even believe the words I was hearing so I know Lauren must have been in shock. I wanted to be there for her, to comfort her, but if it couldn't be me, I was grateful that she was with Kasie and Jeremy, whom Lauren is extremely close to. My brother-in-law serves as youth pastor at his church and loves youth and is such a calming presence in times of trouble.

With every second that passed, it just brought into focus the stark reality that our little boy wasn't ever coming back. As hard as it was to leave him behind at the hospital, we were ready to get to Sadie and Maddie and check on them. My sweet sister-in-law, Tiffany, drove us to her house where our girls had been taken to wait for us. When we told them that their little brother had not made it, that he had passed away, they just fell over on us and quietly cried. They were strangely quiet, and I was worried about how they would be able to deal with this.

From there, Tim and Alison Wildmon drove us to our home. We were all very quiet. My head was spinning. I hated everything about what was happening. I had so many questions racing through my mind. One of which was, what was it going to be like pulling up the drive, past the scene of the accident and walking into our quiet house which is usually so full of life and laughter? But even with all of the questions, all of the fear of the unknown and the tremendous sadness, I can honestly say I could already feel the peace of God covering me almost like a blanket.

When we finally arrived at our house, Zach, Clay Cruse and Greg Johnson had thoughtfully cleaned up the yard and garage for us and had hauled off the dune buggy. So, the house looked just as it usually did, but the feel was eerily different.

However, we didn't really have time to take in just how very different things were because we had some unexpected friends waiting on us as we arrived, so there was a lot of busyness. Really the only things I actually remember about coming home were looking at the stairs and thinking, *Am I really never going to hear Cooper's sweet laughter or see him running down those stairs again?* My friend Alison helped me put away some groceries she had picked up for us. Chris Barker, a friend of ours, looked down and noticed a rock that sat in our living room with Psalm 62:2 carved into it. When he saw it he said, "How true and timely this verse is," and then he read it aloud, "He alone is my rock and my salvation, He is my fortress, I will never be shaken." I remember thinking, when I heard that, *Thank you, Jesus, that you are right here with us.*

For the next week or so, I remember being surrounded by family and friends who were helping us with the girls and just loving us and lifting us up in prayer. However, if I can be real honest, at first I didn't want all of them there because I am a very private person, and when trials come I like to be left alone, I don't like to show my emotions. But it didn't take me long to realize how much we needed each one of them with us. They were all helping in some capacity, whether it was keeping the girls busy, helping us make funeral arrangements, buying clothes for the funeral, or just sitting quietly with us. We never thought something like this would happen to us, but there we were right in the middle of the pain of it all and it was truly wonderful to have people surrounding us during that time. If you ever find yourself in a situation where you can be there for a friend, don't hesitate. You may be just who the Lord uses to bring what that person needs at the right time.

I remember when my sweet momma had to leave to go back to her home, and my sister and her family had to do the same, and how the visits from people became fewer and fewer and then were just rare. That's when the real grieving began. When you get back to the everyday grind of your own life, reality really kicks in.

So, there we were, the five of us, in our now Cooperless world, trying to figure out this new normal. Oh, what I wouldn't give to have his sweaty little self come in from playing hard and catch a whiff of that wonderful, musty little boy smell, or to have one of those unforgettable neck hugs from him that would nearly cut off all the air supply and blood flow to your body because he would squeeze so hard, or just lie in bed with him before school – just a few minutes longer than we should – and cuddle just once more. We all had some special "Cooper" thing we wish we could have back, if only one more time.

It wasn't uncommon for me to panic looking into the rear-view mirror of the car to see we were missing a child. You know, moms, when your heart goes into your throat for that split second when you can't find your child. I would think, *Oh my goodness, where did I leave him?!* Then I would shake my head because I would remember, *Oh yeah,* and I would pray the girls didn't see me do that. Oh, and as the only cook in the house I must confess that, out of habit, I made six plates of food instead of five for months after the accident – that was a devastating moment every day – but I may have been more sad when enough time had passed that five plates became the norm. And I will never forget the first out-of-town trip we took without him, I felt like I physically had cinder blocks on my chest. It was a real physical pain in my body. I didn't want to leave Tupelo, not without him. I knew he wasn't in Tupelo; I knew he was in heaven, but I can't explain it. I just didn't want to go on a trip without him. All of the firsts are truly hard, brutal even. I remember J.J. said once at the end of the day, "Well we are one more day closer to seeing him again," and I thought to myself, *No, it's been another day since the last time I held him.*

Although we had all of these new daily experiences that we had to work through, God was good, and I don't want you to think that the laughter had left our home. We are a fun family, we pack more into life than just about any other family I know, and that hasn't changed. It is just different now. Laughter really is good like a medicine, and we literally found ourselves laughing at different things even days after the accident. It is okay to laugh. It does not mean you aren't hurting. We just serve an awesome God who is able to give us unexplainable joy in the middle of sadness.

God has a purpose and a plan for each one of us. Jeremiah 29:11 assures us: "For I know the plans I have for you says the Lord, plans to prosper you and not to harm you, plans to give you hope and a future."

Now, I don't understand why this happened to us, why the Lord took our sweet Cooper, our beautiful blonde-haired, blue-eyed little man. The precious little boy that I carried inside me for nine months and I had dreamed of my whole life. I sure don't know why and really do wish His plan could have been worked out another way, but the truth is God in all His wisdom has great plans for us and His ways are not our ways. They are higher than our ways and we won't always understand them.

What I do know, is that God is good and His plans are perfect, not painless. He has never left me even for a minute, and He is the peace that passes all understanding. He is still helping me through this grieving process. I thank the Lord that this isn't the end of the story, that eternity is a whole lot longer than this life here on earth, and the best is yet to come! Revelation 21:4 says, "He will wipe every tear from their eyes. There will be no more death, or sorrow or crying or pain. All these things are gone forever."

Oh, how I long for the day when I will get to see my Jesus face to face and be reunited with my sweet Cooper, but until then, I am going to tell everyone I can that there is hope in Jesus! He is good, He is faithful, He is merciful, He is gracious, and the list goes on and on. He has truly blessed me more than I deserve and continues to bless our family with good things. One of the biggest blessings was the gift of Kasie James Jasper who was born almost one year from the day Cooper went home to be with Jesus. She is an incredible little girl who has a love for life that is contagious!

God is the giver of life and of all good things, and He never wastes pain. I know beyond a shadow of a doubt that He could have saved Cooper that day, but He had much different plans. He decided to use a

Melanie holding Cooper just minutes old

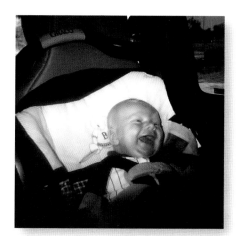

Belly laughing at only two months old

Melanie, her mom, Kandi, and Cooper

Daddy's little
Kentucky
wildcat

One happy baby

Yes, I know
I'm cute.

He could make anything fun – even hanging out in a hotel room with just a couple paper cups and a pair of Daddy's shoes.

Cooper at Aunt Kasie and Uncle Jeremy's wedding

Always smiling

Lauren, Sadie, Maddie, and Cooper – one of our favorite pictures of the kids

Not even two years old and strong enough to pull his sisters in a wagon

Summer fun

He loved his red boots.

Out numbered,
but in control

Cooper as the
Incredible Hulk

Cooper and his
Mawmaw,
Melanie's mom

Cooper and
his Pappy,
Melanie's dad

Big sis, Sadie,
riding Cooper on
the horse

The Jasper Boys

Fun day at the park

Sweet
memories

First tee
ball game

Can you say,
"Excited?"

Grandma Martha
(JJ's mom) with
Cooper and
Maddie

Our little
country boy

Mawmaw and Pappy having fun with the kids

On the set of **Courageous** with Robert Amaya, the "Snake King"

You can be "incredible" even with your mask turned inside out.

Melanie and
her little man

Camping at
Tishomingo
State Park

A whole lot
of cuteness

One happy
daddy

Best buds

What hams …
always ready for
the camera

Celebrating a new
belt in karate

This is what
happens when
you live in a
house with three
big sisters!

What you talkin'
'bout, Willis?

At the wedding of some dear friends of ours

Cooper with his teacher, Lora Garland, and his first trophies

Cooper as the doctor in his school play

Trying to stay
cool on a hot
summer's day

(Left) Fun at Dol-
lywood

Our little super
hero

Play ball!

Relaxing at
Jellystone Park

The Jaspers
February, 2009

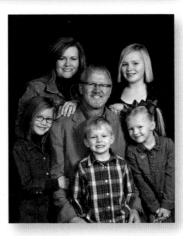

Our precious gift from God,
Kasie James Jasper

little boy to draw many unto Himself. I thank God that Romans 8:28 is true and all things really do work together for good to us that love Him!

O death, where is thy sting?
O grave, where is thy victory?
I CORINTHIANS 15:55 (KJV)

The Funeral

As much as was possible in the midst of the tears and sorrow, Cooper's memorial service was truly a home-going, a celebration of a life lived well. The visitation was on Sunday afternoon at Hope Church in Tupelo, Mississippi. Cooper was dressed in a suit and tie, handsome as could be, and was in the casket at the altar of our church. Hundreds stood in a long line and patiently waited to view the body, hug Melanie and me, and offer tearful condolences.

Sunday evening we retreated to our farm surrounded by family and food provided by loving folks. We tried our best to get some sleep knowing that the funeral on Monday would require every ounce of physical, spiritual and emotional strength.

We had the service at Hope Church instead of the funeral home because we anticipated a large crowd to attend and pay their last respects. Nearly 1,000 people attended to say goodbye to this remarkable little boy who never met a stranger and impacted all who met him.

Long-time friends established a sense of worship with their beautiful music. Randall Murphree played a piano prelude. Tom and Linda Wilson sang as their daughter Katie accompanied them on the acoustic guitar. Later in the service, my uncle, Paul Gatewood, sang "How Great Thou Art."

After the introductory singing, Sam Shaw, then lead pastor of Hope Church, welcomed everyone with these words: "On behalf of J.J. and Melanie and Lauren and Sadie and Maddie and Cooper, I want to thank you for the kindness and the love that you have shown to this family. Scripture says, 'Weep with those who weep.' Hope Church and Lakeview Baptist Church and Academy and American Family Association and American Family Radio, you have done that. Thank you. Thank you for that.

"Samuel Cooper Jasper was five years old when he went home to be with Jesus on Friday, July 17, 2009. Cooper was born on February 24, 2004, in Tupelo to James (J.J.) and Melanie Anderson Jasper. He was a K-4 student at Lakeview Baptist Academy in Tupelo. Cooper was one of the sweetest, kindest boys who ever lived, and he brought joy to everyone he met. He had an infectious smile and a passion for life, and he loved his momma, his daddy and his sisters beyond measure. He earned a yellow belt in karate, and he played baseball. He loved animals, the outdoors and action super heroes. He asked Jesus to come into his life on November 17, 2008, and God is honoring his faithful promise to grant Cooper eternal life."

Pastor Sam proceeded to read Cooper's obituary, then shared these words: "I once had someone tell me, 'On the hardest day of your life, go to the deepest thing you know about God and hang on.' You did that J.J. I don't know if you remember. There in the emergency room you and Melanie were right over your little boy, and you said, 'The Lord gave and the Lord took away. Blessed be the name of the Lord.' You worshiped there. You did it with tears, just like Job did.

"Scripture says in doing that, Job did not sin. Someone came up to me yesterday; he had lost his wife, the funeral service took place here, and he did that. He went into a room and he sat down and said, 'What do I know about God on the worst day of my life?' He wrote these things. 'I know God is good; God is faithful; God is sovereign; nothing catches God off guard; Jesus Christ lives in me; my sins are forgiven; I know for certain I am going to heaven; His Spirit bears witness with my spirit that I am His child; He never makes a mistake; God loves me unconditionally; God uses everything that touches my life for my good; God uses everything that touches my life to accomplish His purpose; God's grace is totally sufficient; God gives us peace in the middle of the storm; God's plans for me are for my welfare and good; God's will for me is good, perfect and acceptable; God heals; God delivers; God sets the captives free; God gives joy in the midst of adversity; God will see me through this storm; God will provide my every need; I don't have to carry my burdens alone with fear or anxiety and worry; I don't have to live in fear of the future; I don't have to live in the shame of my past failures.'

"This is what Scripture says. On the worst day of their life, Mary and Martha came to Jesus and said, 'If You had only been here this wouldn't have happened.'

"Jesus said, 'I am the resurrection and the life. Whoever believes in Me, though he die, yet shall he live. Everyone who lives and believes in Me shall never die. Do you believe this?'

"She said to the Lord, 'I believe you are the Christ, the Son of God who is coming into the world.'

"Scripture says:

> What then should we say to these things? If God is for us, who can be against us?" He who did not spare His own son but gave Him up for us all, how will He not also with Him graciously give us all things? Who shall bring any charge against God's elect? It is God who justifies. Who is to condemn? Christ Jesus is the one who died - more than that, who was raised, who is at the right hand of God, who indeed is interceding for us? Who shall separate us from the love of Christ? Shall tribulation, or distress, or persecution, or famine, or nakedness, or danger, or sword? As it is written, "For Your sake we are being killed all day long. We are regarded as sheep to be slaughtered." No, in all these things, we are more than

conquerors through Him who loved us. For I am sure that neither death, nor life, nor angels, nor rulers, nor things present, nor things to come, nor powers, nor height, nor depth, nor anything else in all creation will be able to separate us from the love of God that is in Christ Jesus our Lord.'"

"One last verse:

I tell you this, brothers, flesh and blood cannot inherit the kingdom of God, nor does the perishable inherit the imperishable. Behold, I tell you a mystery. We shall not all sleep. [It's the Christian word for death.] But, we shall all be changed in a moment, in a twinkling of an eye, at the last trumpet. For the trumpet will sound and the dead will be raised imperishable and we shall be changed. For this perishable body must put on the imperishable and this mortal body must put on immortality. And when the perishable puts on the imperishable, and the mortal puts on the immortality, then shall come to pass the same that is written, death is swallowed up in victory. Oh, death, where is your sting? Oh, grave, where is your victory? The sting of death is sin and the power of sin is the law. But, thanks be to God who gives us the victory through our Lord Jesus Christ. Therefore, my beloved brothers, be steadfast, immovable, always abounding in the work of the Lord because you know that your labor is not in vain in the Lord.

And then Pastor Sam prayed: "Let's pray together. Lord, we are not ashamed of the Gospel. We know it is the power for salvation now and for eternity, for all who believe. By Your grace and mercy You opened the heart of little Cooper to the Gospel and gave him, at a young age, an understanding. You gave him eternal life. He is in Your hands. We have come not to say good-bye but to say until later. We thank You, Lord, that there will come a day when a reunion will take place in the presence of God and the joy will not be able to be contained. But, at this moment, Lord, we grieve, we hurt and we sorrow. You surround us with friends and with family. Lord, there is a deep empty place in our heart, and I pray that over time, through talking and tears, through trusting You, that J.J. and Melanie and their family will find Your healing in that place. Lord, we ask for Your comfort for them. We pray that in these moments that our eyes, though full of tears, be turned to Jesus. We pray it in His name. Amen."

Rev. Robert Garland, pastor of Lakeview Baptist Church and the principal where Cooper attended school, delivered the message. He began by saying, "The Bible tells us in Psalm 139:14, 'I will praise Thee for I am fearfully and wonderfully made.' I think that is a verse that describes Cooper, fearfully and wonderfully made. I've had the opportunity to know the Jaspers for a number of years and opportunity to know Cooper all of his life. This last year I had the opportunity to be his principal at Lakeview Baptist Academy. He was just a joy to have in our school. We've been close to the Jasper family for some time. The thing I remember most about Cooper is how he would just light up the day when you saw him. That smile – there was something about it, when you saw it you couldn't help but know that he had a true joy and a true love for the Lord. He had a true love for life."

He then shared his favorite Cooper story, a cute story about him being in the school play. He then continued: "Cooper was one hundred percent boy. He was just all out. He was just all boy from day one. J.J. wrote something and he asked me to read it. I think this tells you just the kind of boy that Cooper was:

'God gave us a precious gift February 24, 2004, at 11:27 P.M. Samuel Cooper Jasper was born. We were privileged to enjoy five years to know him, love him and be loved by him. Psalm 127:3-5 says, "Sons are a heritage from the Lord, and children are a reward from him. Blessed is the man whose quiver is full of them." Cooper was a blessing. He brought us so much joy and was absolutely a gift from God. Melanie and I wanted you to know a little more about our special little boy. If there was ever such a thing as a perfect child, it was Cooper. Not to take away anything from our wonderful, precious daughters, but Cooper was very, very special. He never gave us a minute's trouble and was a perfect balance in almost every way as a son, a little brother, student and friend. He was a remarkable boy in every way.

'From early on, Melanie and I were convinced that he had a call from God on his life. Certainly the Lord's hand was on him. His desire to obey and to please the Lord would rival that of many adults. Cooper had the discipline of a Marine, an incredible sense of humor, and he absolutely had a servant's heart. He lived life with so much zeal and energy, he smiled constantly and brought joy to everyone he met. He was so very kind, generous, helpful, grateful, and thoughtful. To God be the glory! Once again, he was practically a perfect child.

'Cooper's first word was "Backhoe." At only 15 months old he taught himself how to snap his fingers. Then he taught his big sisters. To this day our daughters can snap their fingers because someone who couldn't even talk showed them how. Imagine that!

'When Daddy was away on a trip, Cooper would proclaim that he would be the man of the house. His best friend was Aaron Mangum. He earned a yellow belt in Karate. He played baseball. He loved to swing, swim, jump on the trampoline, enjoyed animals, and loved to play with his toys. He especially liked action super heroes. He was artistic and very smart. His greatest joy was the love he had for his parents, his sisters and his Lord Jesus Christ. Almost daily, complete strangers would comment on how special he was.

'Cooper impacted many lives in so few years. Cooper was all boy. Recently he told his mother, "I think I like baseball better than karate."

Knowing how much he enjoyed karate, Melanie asked him, "Why?" Cooper said, "I like the way my cleats sound when I am walking on the parking lot." We crammed a lot of life into five years. His last week and a half on earth he shot fire works, went swimming, played with his dog, rode his bike, rode the wave runner, and flew in an airplane with his dad. Cooper was laughing, riding in a dune buggy when the Lord called him home. His last words were, "Flame on!" It was something he would say to make Daddy go faster.

'Thank you for your love, support and prayers for our family. Certainly this is every parent's worst nightmare. Personally, I want to say I'm sorry. Humanly speaking I was responsible and take the blame for the accident. I was driving the dune buggy when it flipped. Our faith and trust, however, is in the loving sovereign God who, according to His word, has each of our days numbered. There is an appointed time for each of us to die. We're trusting the Lord to someway, somehow get glory from this terrible tragedy. Thank you again for your love and continued prayers. Thank you for helping us celebrate the life and home-going of Samuel Cooper Jasper. We'll miss him more than we can say. We'll see him again. Right now, at this very moment he is in heaven with Jesus.'

"If you will allow me to add something else to read, my wife, Lora, was Cooper's teacher this last year. From him being at school and in her class, we got very close to him. This is something that my wife, Lora Garland, wrote. She writes, 'J.J. and Melanie asked me if I would be willing to say a few words about their son, Cooper, since I was his teacher this past year. I know that teachers are not supposed to have favorites, but I have to confess, Cooper was definitely a student that I would have picked as my favorite. He was such a joy to teach, and I'm thankful to have had that privilege. Cooper was the most precious and beautiful child, and I loved him dearly. So obedient, polite, well behaved and a tribute to his wonderful parents.

'As a student he was very bright and loved learning. He was a perfectionist in everything that he did. There were times that he would literally tear a hole in his paper from erasing so much. His paper had to be just right. Cooper loved getting stickers and smiley faces on his papers, and loved for me to write "Super Dooper Cooper" on his work sheets. At his K-4 graduation and awards ceremony in May, Cooper was awarded a trophy for being star student in his class. He was so proud of that trophy. His parents told me that he went to sleep with it that night and carried it with him everywhere for the next few days. I'm now so thankful that I chose Cooper for that award. It is always a hard decision to make because I am blessed with so many good boys and girls. But I believe that Cooper was very deserving of that award.

'Cooper was not only dearly loved by his teacher but by all of his classmates and the entire staff and student body of Lakeview Baptist Academy. The junior high and high school lunch period overlapped with my class lunchtime. So, for a brief period we would share the lunchroom with them. Every day, as the older students would come into the cafeteria, Cooper would get so excited to see the big kids. I can still hear them call his name, "Cooper," as the older boys would give him high fives, and the older girls would hug him and kiss his sweet little cheeks. Sometimes Cooper would tease them by wiping off their kisses, knowing he would get more. He was such a love bug and an affectionate boy.

'The thing I remember most about Cooper was his vibrant smile. He always had a smile on his face and thoroughly enjoyed life. He was definitely a bright spot in my day as he was for others. Cooper was very artistic and would draw some truly amazing pictures for a boy his age. I remember him coming up to my desk many times with a picture he had made for me. Most of the time it was a picture of one of his action heroes. But, sometimes it was a picture of the two of us, Cooper and me. Other times it was a picture of my family, including our dog, Peanut. Again, that was just like Cooper to include everyone in his little world. Cooper didn't leave anyone out. He was a friend to all. Cooper also loved to sing. He was adorable in our graduation program as he sang his little heart out. He didn't miss a beat. I imagine he has been enjoying singing with the angels these past few days as he entered heaven's gates. Although my heart is greatly saddened by his loss, I know that Cooper is safe in the arms of Jesus. That gives me great peace.

'They say that teachers touch lives forever. But in this case it is the other way around. Samuel Cooper Jasper has touched this teacher's life forever. He has touched my life in more ways than I can mention. Although he is gone he will not be forgotten. I shall cherish the memory of this precious child of God forever. Mrs. Lora Garland'

"Thank you for allowing me to read this letter from my wife, Lora."

"I can remember watching as Cooper played in the gym at school and thinking, *That fellow is just as tough as boot leather.* He was all boy. And yet, he was tender and loving. He had a compassionate side to him. I think that is a tribute to his mom and his three sisters. He had four girls at home. He could melt your heart with that smile. He did everything with all his might. He had a genuine love for his friends, for his sisters, for his mom, for his dad and for the Lord.

"My daughter and I were reflecting, and she reminded me of this. The kids would come down to recess. Maddie's class would take recess at the same time that Cooper's class would take recess. They would meet in the gym. When their eyes met they just would light up and they would run across that gym and embrace each other as though they hadn't seen each other in years. Can you imagine the reunion in heaven? What a wonderful glad reunion that will be. Cooper lived an abundant life. You saw that in the slide show. He did so many things. He loved super heroes. I remember being at their house one time, and he came out, and he was dressed up as the Incredible Hulk. A few minutes later he would be dressed up as Spider Man. A few minutes later he would be one of the Incredibles or the Fantastic Four. He just loved super heroes. But, by far, his favorite Super Hero was his dad. He went to sleep in this life in the arms of his daddy, his Super Hero. But, he woke up in the arms of the greatest hero a man can have and that is Jesus Christ.

"He loved Bible stories in school. My wife would tell Bible stories and show picture cards. He, like any other child, wanted to be right up front where he could see. He would say, 'Teacher, I can't see. He has moved in front of me and won't get out of the way.' Can you imagine now how much he is enjoying heaven's Super Heroes, as he gets to sit and talk to David and hear him tell first hand what it was like to kill Goliath, to kill that bear or that lion with his bare hands? Imagine as he is talking to Daniel, and he says, 'What was it like in the lion's den?' He's not just hearing a story that is being relayed from the Bible by his teacher or parents. He is hearing it first hand and loving every minute of it.

"Melanie has shared with my wife how she would often pray at night, 'Lord, let Cooper grow up to be a mighty warrior for you.' Melanie, I know that you were thinking of when he became a man. He's a mighty warrior in his life.

"I understand that Lauren was just at camp. The theme for camp was 'One Phone Call Will Flip Your World.' It was said several times during the week at camp. On Friday night she got that one phone call. But that one phone call had a ripple effect that led to numerous decisions being made for Christ. Cooper died a mighty warrior, and God is using him. God will continue to use him.

"I want to draw your attention back to the verse that I read at the beginning. Most people have heard this verse and know this, especially the part of the verse that I read, 'I will praise Thee for I am fearfully and wonderfully made.' But the verse goes on. The Bible says, 'Marvelous are Thy works and that my soul knoweth right well.' Marvelous are Thy works. We serve an awesome God. We sang that a few minutes ago. We serve a God whose works are marvelous. We serve a God who doesn't make mistakes. We serve a God that, in those marvelous works, He gave us Cooper to enjoy. Not only though did He give us Cooper;

many years ago gave His only begotten Son to come to this earth and live for just 33 years, go to the cross and shed His precious blood, and die for the sins of mankind. He died for your sins, and He died for my sins. He died that we might live. In doing that he did one of the most marvelous works that could be done. He made a way for us to be reunited with Cooper in heaven.

"Cooper knew the Lord as his Savior. You have that same opportunity to trust the Lord. You have that same opportunity to accept Christ as your personal Savior and be prepared for eternity. It would be a shame for anyone to leave here today and not know the Jesus that Cooper invited into his heart.

"Most often, in situations like this, questions are asked: A missionary friend that was serving God on the mission field had a death in his family. He had to come home from that field for a while. While he was at the funeral someone walked up to him and handed him a small piece of a jigsaw puzzle. On the back of that jigsaw puzzle piece there was a reference. It was Romans 8:28, 'We know that all things work together for good to them that love God, to them who are the called according to His purpose.' He looked at it a little bit puzzled for a moment. The man who handed it to him said, 'We can't see the whole picture. But God can. God can.' The piece of the puzzle that we see oftentimes is a blank piece of the puzzle. Oftentimes it is a hard piece of the puzzle for us to comprehend. Often times that piece brings us heartache or it brings us tears. But we don't see the whole picture. God sees the whole picture and God's picture is beautiful. Our part is to trust Him to finish that puzzle in our lives. Though on this earth, on this side, we may not understand, and we may not see all that God intended to do with the life of Cooper and with his passing. But God makes no mistakes. He knows what He is doing. The words of a song say, 'My life I give to You, oh Lord. Use me, I pray. May I magnify Thy precious name in all I do and say. Let me trust You in the valley dark, as well as in the light.

Knowing You will always lead me. Your will is always right.

'I know God makes no mistakes. He leads in every path I take, along the way that is leading me to home. Though at times my heart would break there is purpose in every change He makes, that others would see my life and know that God makes no mistakes.'"

Bro. Rob concluded with a stirring prayer, then came down from behind the podium, walked over to us, and handed us a puzzle piece with Romans 8:28 written on the back.

Eric Pittman, another dear friend, sang a moving hymn of praise. The service concluded with the congregation singing the classic children's song, "Jesus Loves Me."

Pallbearers included, Greg Johnson, Clay Cruse, Zach Anderson, Durick Hayden, Jeremy Ulmer, Randall Murphree, Paul Gatewood and honorary pallbearer, Kenny Kessinger. Clay inspired the pallbearers to write "flame on" across their knuckles with a magic marker. The Tupelo Police Department had provided a full police escort. Several patrol cars had "flame on" written on the windows. Those small, thoughtful gestures meant more than we can express.

As we traveled across town to the cemetery, through a maze of thoughts and many tears, I remember how impressed I was to watch cars pull over to show respect as the funeral procession passed by. I'm grateful to live in America and in the South where respect, manners and tradition still matter.

At the graveside, I remember getting out of the car, then stopping and waiting on Cooper to get out of the Suburban to join us. There would be many more incidents of denial, one of the common stages of grief. There is part of your brain that bargains with God, and you think someway, somehow, God will change the rules of the universe, just this once, and Cooper will walk through the door, and everything will be back to normal.

Steve Hallman – pastor, educator and long-time family friend – spoke to the immediate family at the graveside service. After some introductory words of condolence, Steve said, "In the next few weeks and months people will come up to you with good intentions and tell you that in time you'll get over this. They mean well, but it's simply not true. You'll never get over this. This is not a wound that heals, it's an amputation. Just like someone who's lost an arm or leg or a hand, you have to find a new normal. You're going to have to find a new way to do life without Cooper. You'll never get over this … but you will get through it with God's help."

It took many months for the reality to sink in that, accept it or not, this was our new normal.

Steve offered more wise words and condolences in the short service as we said our goodbyes to our precious, sweet boy at the Tupelo Memorial Gardens Cemetery. If you go there today you'll find his headstone engraved with these words: "His love for life and his love for Jesus was as contagious as his sweet smile."

We left the cemetery and went to Cafe 212 where owners, Jason and Amanda Hayden, closed their cafe to regular business and prepared lunch for our family and a lot of close friends. The gift of their time and loss of revenue was just one more of the countless acts of love that kept us going. Jason is the son of Durick and Debbie Hayden, who lost Jason's brother, Chris, in an accident several years prior. The Haydens could truly empathize with our grief, and they, along with other faithful friends, have walked with us every step of the way through this journey.

Brothers and sisters, I do not consider myself yet to have taken hold of it. But one thing I do: Forgetting what is behind and straining toward what is ahead, I press on toward the goal to win the prize for which God has called me heavenward in Christ Jesus.

PHILIPPIANS 3:13-14

12

Guilt and Regret

I didn't check on Cooper the night before he died, even though I promised him I would. When it was his bedtime, he appeared at the stair rail, looked down into the living room, and asked if I would please come see him before I went to bed. In all his innocence, Cooper reappeared several more times saying, "You promise you'll come check on me, Daddy?"

I told him I would, but I didn't. It was my very last opportunity to tuck him in and snuggle with my best little buddy, and I missed it. You can only imagine how many times that scene has been repeated over and over in my mind.

After Cooper's death I struggled with regrets about little things like that. Simple requests he made that I had denied. These have brought me so much pain. And these memories brought something else: guilt.

One dictionary defines guilt as: "1. Awareness of wrongdoing: an awareness of having done wrong or committed a crime, accompanied by feelings of shame and regret. 2. A feeling of responsibility or remorse for some offense, crime, wrong, whether real or imagined."

The thing about guilt is that, even when it recedes for a while, it returns with a vengeance. It was difficult to even think about Cooper without the guilt coming, too. Guilt made it hard to grieve.

The elephant in the room, of course, was the fact that I was driving the dune buggy when the rollover claimed the life of our only son. It happened on my watch. I was the one in charge.

Moreover, so much that happened that day seemed to be my fault. I'm the one who suggested that Melanie go into town to get a little break. She was hesitant but I insisted. It was my idea to ride the dune buggy after the lawnmower suddenly quit. Cooper was perfectly content riding his little bicycle round and round in circles in the garage. Later, he was happy enough when we played together on our swing set.

There were additional thoughts to compound my guilt. Not only was I driving but obviously I was going too fast when I made the decision to turn sharply, floor it and do a "donut." If I had been puttering along and hadn't spun around, Cooper would still be here.

There's never a limit to the amount of blame when guilt is burrowing into your brain like a cancer. I remember that fateful day like it was yesterday – that antsy feeling I get when I feel the need to cram too much activity into a single day, hurrying and jumping from activity to activity. My entire life I've been accused of being hyperactive or a little ADHD. I'll admit it's hard for me to sit still for very long in one place or stay engaged in whatever task is at hand. I tend to bore easily, lose focus, and dart from thing to thing.

I've always enjoyed speed and adventure. I always liked extreme sports. I was a wrestler in high school and grew up riding dirt bikes and horses. I've owned many different kinds of vehicles and always wanted to see how fast they would go or how high I could get them off the ground. I lived life on the edge. Before I was a Christian I drank a lot of alcohol – adding to the dangerous life I was living. I can't tell you how many times when I was young, friends would walk away from me and my rowdy buddies and declare, "Let's get out of here, you guys are going to kill someone or kill yourselves."

Only seconds after the accident those words were ringing in my ears. There was a kind of crushing, suffocating guilt that accompanied them.

It haunts me to wonder: Did that character flaw of mine prove fatal to my son? I've endured many sleepless nights wondering if Cooper would be safe and alive today if I wasn't the way I am. Why couldn't I just have continued enjoying what we were doing, instead of getting in the dune buggy? When you flitter and dart from this to that, I think you miss the opportunity to savor what's right in front of you. When we live life at a frantic pace, I fear we lose some of the peace and joy that is to be found.

Then came those voices in my mind, echoing the disapproval of my stern father years ago, when I would accidentally drop something, spill something or knock something over: "How could you be so careless? What were you thinking? Why weren't you paying attention? Now look what you've done! It's broken beyond repair!" Those voices were screaming condemnation in my head while I was asking God to help my dying son and begging Him for a miracle.

I've gone over it thousands of times in my mind, especially in the first weeks after the accident. The progression of "what-ifs" plagued me. What if the lawn mower hadn't stopped working? What if I hadn't bought the dune buggy in the first place? What if we hadn't bought the farm and moved to the country?

In my mind there was a futile attempt to "fix" the timeline. Go to the exact place where the breakdown occurred. Find the problem in the sequence that caused the chain reaction that led to my son's death. Surely there is an exact spot to assign the blame, to identify and obsess over and declare: "Aha! There it is! There is the place in the timeline that if it had not occurred our lives would be normal and our son would be alive."

The problem with that is there is no way to find the exact spot to "fix" the timeline. There's no one place to point. You say to yourself: *If we hadn't bought the farm, if we hadn't gotten married, if we hadn't had children, if our parents hadn't met and married in the first place – then we wouldn't be in this dark and terrible place of suffering.* I suppose others, like me, have lamented regarding a fatal accident and tortured themselves mentally wondering. *If only I had driven a different route that day, if only*

I had left five minutes sooner, if only ...

I believe you can drive yourself crazy dwelling on the "what-ifs" or "if-onlys" or the "should've, would've and could've" scenarios trying to fix the timeline.

Add to all this guilt the accusations in your soul that the tragedy was a result of sin. Is God repaying me for some terrible thing I've done in the past or something I'm failing to do? Condemnation adds to the torment of guilt.

For the documentary **Flame On**, we asked Dr. James C. Dobson, founder of Family Talk, if he would record some comments, and what he said was so very helpful to me, especially about guilt. He said that when someone has suffered a tragedy, the worst thing a friend can do is blame it on sin in the life of the grieving soul.

"That's ridiculous," he said. "What you are doing is you are cutting the person off from the relationship with the Lord at the time that they need it the most and they need Him the most."

That's what the devil tries to do. Scripture teaches that Satan is the accuser of the brethren. So it's the devil's job description to perch on our shoulder and whisper taunting jabs to blame and condemn us.

"J.J. would not have hurt a cell of that little boy's body," Dr. Dobson said. "He would have laid down his life for Cooper. So, the issue of responsibility and blame and all that is a tool that Satan uses to discourage you and to drive a wedge between you and God. Don't go down that path."

If logic alone could protect from guilt, I wouldn't have been so tortured by it. On the basis of logic, I could have answered: I don't drink alcohol anymore – and haven't since becoming a Christian. I'm no longer the foolish young man who was reckless and tried stupid stunts for the thrill or attention. I've mellowed considerably over the years.

As far as our children were concerned, Melanie and I were always overly cautious with them. Yes, I was driving the dune buggy the day my son died, but I wasn't showing off. I wasn't driving wild and crazy. Cooper was buckled in securely. We were driving on a straight stretch up and down a dirt lane in our pasture. A dad and his boy having fun. A father and son making memories. It was only after we were through riding that I turned the wheel and floored it and was going to spin around on level ground then head to the house. It was an accident.

Yet guilt does not surrender its grip so easily. Logic is a two-edged sword: It defends – and accuses: "You weren't content to swing on the swings. You were going a little too fast or the dune buggy wouldn't have flipped. You were the one who turned the wheel. You caused it to flip. You killed your son."

Maybe you are reading this, and you are feeling the weight of guilt, too. Maybe you were involved in someone else's injury or death. Maybe you were showing off or drunk or on drugs or sleep deprived or negligent or …. Fill in the blank. And now you also feel the dagger of condemnation in your heart.

You can't un-ring a bell. We can't undo something that's been done. We can't change the past – we can't turn back the clock even a few seconds to make something turn out differently.

We need something more than explanations and logic. We certainly can't simply choose to ignore the guilt and pain, because they just won't go away.

The very next day after the accident I asked my friend Clay Cruse, who had stayed up all night at our home, to walk down our gravel driveway out to the pasture. I wanted to go to the scene of the accident and see if there was a hump in the pasture or something that caused the dune buggy to flip over instead of just spinning around like so many times before.

As we walked Clay asked me, "Do you think the Lord could have prevented the dune buggy from rolling over?"

"Of course," I answered.

He continued, "Do you think He was on the job, watching, fully aware and completely in control?"

"Yes," I answered.

"Do you think there is anything impossible for God?" he asked.

"No."

"So, you think God was watching yesterday? He had not wandered off, and if He had wanted to, He could have prevented the dune buggy from rolling over and spared Cooper's life?"

"Yes, yes!" I answered, a bit frustrated. "How many more ways can I answer yes?"

Clay was undaunted as he continued asking me over and over from slightly different angles: "Do you think God could have intervened and changed the outcome?" Despite my growing annoyance, he asked me the same question nearly a dozen times, forcing me to hear my answer. He would say, "Are you sure? Do you really believe that? What I hear you saying is you believe God was completely in charge, completely in control, and He could've kept Cooper alive?" And I continued answering yes.

Finally with a commanding boldness Clay declared: "Then God is more responsible for this than you! You are just a man. He is God. He made you. He made Cooper. He is God; we're not. Heaven and earth belong to God and He alone decides who lives and dies!"

Clay finally demanded that I not shoulder the guilt, that I not accept full blame. He said that I couldn't go through life blaming myself and beating myself up. Especially not when God was there and could've reached down with His little finger and spared Cooper's life.

Those bold words, less than 24 hours after the accident, were a healing balm on my heart, emotionally and spiritually, and gave me a fresh perspective. It takes a special friend to speak words of truth into your life at just the right time – like apples of gold in settings of silver.

Dr. Dobson later concurred in additional insights from **Flame On**. "Guilt is kind of irrational," he said. "You know that God does not hold the person accountable for a mistake or an accident that no one could have foreseen."

He was so right about the emotional nature of what I was going through. It was irrational. There was so much I couldn't figure out, but I was so desperate to make sense of our tragedy.

John 10:10 says, "The thief comes only to steal and kill and destroy; I came that they may have life, and have it abundantly." When I read that and compare it alongside verses of God's sovereignty, I sometimes vacillate. Did Satan kill Cooper and take him from us? Or was this God's plan all along? Or did God allow it to happen? Certainly nothing happens without God allowing it. Everything has to pass through the filter of God's love and His will.

"You should not try to come up with simplistic answers to profound questions that involve the very heart and motivation of God," Dr. Dobson said, even though the "why" question has plagued every human being who has ever lived.

"We all ask that question," he said. "We have reason to ask it because we go through difficulties and moments when the pieces don't fit, when you can't make sense out of what is happening to you. So, we all ask. I draw comfort from the fact that even Jesus asked when he was on the cross, 'My God, My God, why have You forsaken Me?"

God rarely answers that "why" question, Dr. Dobson insisted. In the Bible, Job suffered terribly and asked the Lord deep and penetrating questions – brilliant questions. But he got no answers. Why not? Dr. Dobson said, "Because God will not be accountable to man." Period.

"In the case of little Cooper who died at five years of age, no one can answer the 'why' question," he said, adding, "You can put a thousand theologians in a church and keep them there for six months talking about the 'why' question and they are not going to come up with it."

So then what do we do? I've got questions still. I understand what Dr. Dobson is saying: I won't have all the answers until I get to heaven.

None of us will. But I still get ambushed by guilt and regret. I still hurt. What is my answer right now? I need help now. When I'm in heaven, I'm not even sure I'll ask the "why" question, because I'll no longer be in pain!

The answer came out of my mouth almost without my noticing it. While we were filming **Flame On**, the question was posed to me, "How do you handle the guilt and the grief?" I just blurted my answer out: "It's going to take a lifetime of grace."

There it was: grace. That word appears so many times in the Bible, and yet do we know what it means? Grace is the power of God working in us to accomplish what we cannot do on our own.

When the Apostle Paul was suffering through a great trial, he prayed three times and asked the Lord to remove it. All three times, God said, "No." There was no explanation about why not; there was only this statement to Paul: "My grace is sufficient for you" (2 Corinthians 12:9).

We sent the raw footage of our initial **Flame On** interview to our good friends, Christian recording artists Steve and Annie Chapman, to get their insights and include them as an extra feature for the film. Later, as they were being interviewed, Steve commented:

"J.J. said something [in the raw footage] ... that struck me deep in my heart. He said it in response to all of that grief. J.J. said, 'I'm going to need a lifetime of grace,' and when I heard that – you know I'm a songwriter – I heard the cry of a man's heart. I said this needs to be in a song. I've never heard anyone say that before. And so I almost ran to my desk and grabbed a piece of paper, and the words just almost tumbled out of my heart onto that paper: 'He's gonna need grace for a lifetime not just an hour or a day. Grace for a lifetime to go with him all the way. Until he leaves that sorrow behind, he's gonna need grace for a lifetime.'

"And of course the natural progression for me in the second verse was to talk about all the rest of us who have those same regrets and those same feelings and those same emotions. How many of us are going to need that same grace – not just for an hour or a day, but for a lifetime?" [4]

The grace of God is available to help us all through our troubles, our pain, our regrets – and, yes, our guilt.

As Dr. Dobson said, "God says He is close to the broken hearted; He will not leave us; and He sticks closer than a brother."

Our task in this life, then, is to keep trusting in God and His love for us. "You can trust Him even when you can't track Him or understand His purposes," Dr. Dobson said.

One day our toil and trouble in this life, our sorrow and pain, will be over. "The sovereignty of God will bring things right," Dr. Dobson said. "We know that because the Scripture tells us. Someday we will be together again. J.J. and his wife and Cooper will be there in that reunion."

Until then, we rely on the grace of God to get us home. Grace for a lifetime.

If we confess our sins, He is faithful and just to forgive us our sins, and to cleanse us from all unrighteousness

1 JOHN 1:9 (KJV)

13

Forgiveness

Melanie was the judge and jury in our marriage regarding Cooper's death. She held my heart in her hands. If she had declared me guilty for our son's death, if she had pointed the finger and accused me, I never would have survived. I'm convinced I would not have made it.

She could easily have chained me to my guilt. After all, as I've said, I was in charge – it was on my watch – when her baby, her only son, died. I've never seen a closer relationship between a mother and son. Look what I took from her. No one would have blamed her if she had required me to pay for this tragedy every remaining day of our lives together.

But she didn't. Immediately after the accident, Melanie arrived home from the store and saw Cooper lying on the ground next to our house with the paramedics giving him CPR. She collapsed right there in the driveway. I went to her, cradled her and tried to console her as best I could. They carefully loaded Cooper in the ambulance and strongly suggested we ride in a patrol car and follow, allowing the EMTs in the back to do their work.

In the sheriff's car, Melanie offered forgiveness immediately. As I repeatedly apologized, she interrupted and said, "It was an accident. I know you love Cooper. There is nothing to forgive. You didn't do this on purpose. I know you would lay your life down for him. It was an accident."

After our return from the hospital, we sat around our home with emotions alternating between shock, denial, and disbelief. We were continually asking, "Why?" But besides all this there was something else going on inside me as well. I would fall into a cycle of dropping my head in my hands and tearfully begging my family to forgive me. This process seemed to repeat itself every 30 minutes or so. Melanie was so gracious and forgiving and would say all of the right things and repeat it each time I broke down and started to beg for forgiveness again.

Regarding my part in Cooper's death, Melanie has never – not once – ever brought it up. Every day, many times throughout the day, I would have meltdowns and she would repeat her total unconditional love and forgiveness for me – and she would mean it! It has been an amazing thing to witness and an amazing gift to receive. It was as if she handed me a key to a dark and lonely cell of guilt, shame, and regret, and I was able to unlock the cell door, walk out, and be completely free. I now know what receiving true forgiveness looks like and feels like. If she had held it over my head just a little bit, I wouldn't be able to heal, our marriage would have been strained immensely, and we wouldn't be able to grieve well. What a true demonstration of love and forgiveness. I see Jesus in my wife, Melanie, every day.

In his short story "Capital of the World," Ernest Hemingway tells about a broken relationship between a Spanish father and his teenage son, Paco. The boy ran away from home and went to Madrid. His distraught father looked everywhere for him.

In desperation, the father placed an ad in the Madrid newspaper that read, "Dear Paco, meet me in front of the Hotel Montana tomorrow at noon. All is forgiven. Love, Papa." The next day 800 hopeful young men named Paco were gathered at the meeting place!

Everyone, everywhere desperately needs forgiveness – whether they know it or not. The need for forgiveness is universal. But why?

God made the universe, and He made it a certain way. There are certain things we can change and certain things we can't. If I break a window at my house, I can go to the hardware store and buy a new one and replace it. But there are a lot of things we do that can't be fixed. Hurtful words can't be taken back once they've been spoken; hurtful deeds can't be undone.

You've no doubt seen a television show or movie where someone is in charge of a rare antique vase or priceless painting. You watch nervously as they stumble and fall or knock over the priceless heirloom and then watch in horror as it crashes to pieces. It is something so rare and valuable that you can't put a price tag on it, and it absolutely can never, ever, be replaced.

That's how I felt immediately after the dune buggy rolled over – times one million. The combination of shock and disbelief was magnified beyond what I can explain. At first I thought, *This cannot be happening! This isn't real!* Nothing this awful, this catastrophic and final, could have just taken place in the blink of an eye. There is always a reset button, isn't there? You can always fix anything if you try hard enough, can't you? Someway, somehow, we can turn back the clock – if only for a moment or so – and have a do-over. I was thinking, *Please, God, oh, God, please say this just didn't happen, please let this be a horrible, terrible nightmare!*

Yet the universe doesn't work that way, and because life is the way it is, forgiveness is a necessity for each and every person. We will all break precious things and speak hurtful words and do things that cause others pain. Forgiveness is the only option, because things that can't be undone can't be undone. They can only be forgiven.

Forgiveness is at the very heart of the Bible. Forgiveness is God's answer to the problem of guilt. Death seems to amplify guilt, because you wish you had done or said more to the deceased while they were alive. Also, blame is often assigned when someone dies. I'm told that many marriages fail when a child dies. I haven't taken a survey or done research, but my guess is that one parent blaming the other could destroy the marriage.

Why does the Bible say we all need forgiveness? Some very familiar

Bible verses make it clear:

"For all have sinned, and come short of the glory of God" (Romans 3:23 KJV).

"For the wages of sin is death; but the gift of God is eternal life through Jesus Christ our Lord" (Romans 6:23 KJV).

"But God demonstrates His own love for us in this: While we were still sinners, Christ died for us" (Romans 5:8).

Because of the fall of man through Adam and Eve's disobedience in the Garden of Eden, we are born sinners. As these verses emphasize, we all are sinners, we all have sinned, and eternal death is our recompense – our wages. It is what we have earned; it is what we will receive.

However, God, who is rich in mercy, provided a solution for our sin. He sent His only Son, Jesus, to be born of a virgin; He lived a sinless life and then willingly died on the cross in payment for our sins. The righteous requirements of a Holy God were met completely because of the birth, life, death, crucifixion, and resurrection of our Lord and Savior, Jesus Christ. As Romans 5:8 says, God did this while we were sinners. We did not earn this amazing salvation, because we were already doomed. It was accomplished without us and despite us.

When we accept God's plan of salvation, turn from our sins (when we repent), and turn to the Lord to believe Him and put our trust in Him, then we are born again (John 3:1-5).

It is a glorious experience to realize your need for God, to humble yourself, repent of your sins, and receive Jesus Christ into your heart and life by faith. This is clarified in Ephesians 2:8-10: "For by grace are ye saved through faith; and that not of yourselves: it is the gift of God: Not of works, lest any man should boast. For we are His workmanship, created in Christ Jesus unto good works, which God hath before ordained that we should walk in them" (KJV).

Dealing with our sin is our greatest need, and salvation is the greatest thing that can happen to a person. It is the most important decision we can make.

However, the forgiveness we receive from God when we trust in Christ is really just the beginning. The work of forgiveness continues to expand in our lives. Even when we become Christians and experience God's forgiveness, we then begin to wrestle with forgiving others. But the Bible is filled with verses commanding us to forgive:

"Bear with each other and forgive one another if any of you has a grievance against someone. Forgive as the Lord forgave you" (Colossians 3:13).

"And forgive us our debts, as we also have forgiven our debtors" (Matthew 6:12).

"For if you forgive other people when they sin against you, your heavenly Father will also forgive you. But if you do not forgive others their sins, your Father will not forgive your sins" (Matthew 6:14-15).

When we don't forgive, we hold a grudge; but holding a grudge is like letting someone live rent free in your heart and head. When we release resentment and forgive people, it's like releasing someone from a prison cell only to discover that the prisoner is you! Forgiveness doesn't excuse the behavior of the ones who hurt you. Instead forgiveness prevents their behavior from destroying your heart.

Corrie ten Boom was a Christian during World War II. Corrie, along with her sister and father, hid Jews from the Nazis, but they were caught. For punishment they were sent to Ravensbruck, a Nazi concentration camp. Her sister and father died there, but Corrie was later released. As we might expect, she struggled with bitterness against those who had hurt her so badly. She realized she had to forgive those wicked men.

Corrie ten Boom likened forgiveness to letting go of a bell rope. If you have ever seen a country church with a bell in the steeple, you will remember that to get the bell ringing you have to tug a while. Once it has begun to ring, you merely maintain the momentum. As long as you keep pulling, the bell keeps ringing. She said forgiveness is letting go of the rope. It is just that simple, but when you let go, the bell keeps ringing. Momentum is still at work. However, if you keep your hands off the rope, the bell will begin to slow and eventually stop.

When you decide to forgive, the old feelings of unforgiveness may continue for a while. After all, the sins committed against you and the resulting pain have lots of momentum. But if you make your decision to forgive, the power of that unforgiveness will begin to weaken. Eventually the clanging bell will be still. Forgiveness is letting go of the "rope" of retribution.[5]

Romans 13:8-10 says, "Owe no one anything, except to love each other, for the one who loves another has fulfilled the law. For the commandments, 'You shall not commit adultery, You shall not murder, You shall not steal, You shall not covet,' and any other commandment, are summed up in this word: 'You shall love your neighbor as yourself.' Love does no wrong to a neighbor; therefore love is the fulfilling of the law" (ESV).

Forgiving yourself is sometimes just as difficult as forgiving others. Just as it is often hard to "let go" of the sin committed by others, it is hard to let go of the sins we commit. We sometimes believe others should continue to "pay" for what they've done to us; we also believe that we should pay for what we have done.

I kept having guilt-ridden meltdowns, but a real turning point came just days after Cooper's death. Lauren, our oldest daughter – who was then 13 years old – reminded me that they all loved me and that I was forgiven. But I just couldn't accept that forgiveness. As I ignored her pleadings and continued to spiral down in self pity and remorse, she came across the room with a holy boldness and grabbed me by the shoulders. She literally shook me and said, "Stop this! Look at me, Dad; look me in the eyes! You loved Cooper! We all know that you love us, and you are always careful. You were just having fun with your son. It was an accident, Dad. Please get that through your head. It was an accident! Please stop torturing yourself. Please let this go. You have to forgive yourself and let this go!" Lauren probably doesn't even remember doing that, but it certainly was a breakthrough for me.

As I've reflected on my struggles with forgiveness, I think I've begun to see the root beneath the poisoned tree: I could not forgive myself because I struggle with being a very forgiving person with others. This fact made Lauren's exhortation even more amazing, because I was not always quick to forgive her, even for small blunders. As the oldest, we were often more strict with her. It seems we make all of our parenting mistakes on the oldest child.

I'm also more inclined to give someone the third degree regarding a mistake: "Show me exactly where you were standing. How were you holding it? How could you have done a better job?" Blah, blah, blah. Realizing how petty I can be and how prone I am to nit-pick concerning Lauren and how bold she was to offer unconditional love, well, it was a much needed gift from God and the timing couldn't have been more perfect.

The fact that Melanie and my daughters completely forgave me was important to me, especially when you consider how I'm wired. When it comes to resentment, let's just say I come by that character trait honestly. The kin folk on my father's side of our family are notorious for holding grudges. They have turned, "I told you so's," into an art form. They seem to continually struggle with bitterness and resentment. We don't do well with forgiveness. So if heredity holds true, then it's easy to understand why unfortunately, I constantly have to battle to keep from leaning to the dark side. This is difficult to confess, but you can ask my wife and kids and they will confirm this character flaw in me.

What I am trying to say is if the shoe had been on the other foot, I shudder to think how I would have responded. I often don't do well with tiny offenses. I make mountains out of mole hills and constantly struggle with just letting things go when it comes to being able to forgive and forget. Even regarding little blunders, I sometimes sound like a broken record. I can't seem to control it. (Since I'm confessing that sin, please pray for me that I can be victorious in that area.)

Melanie is the exact opposite. I don't think I've ever seen anyone who so easily forgives and forgets. I'm that guy that keeps a record of wrongs and will probably bring it up in an argument years down the road. Melanie, to her credit, never does. It's amazing to watch how much grace she has in that area. She just refuses to stay mad or harbor the slightest resentment or unforgiveness toward anyone!

Many times since Cooper died, I have considered the magnitude of Melanie's forgiveness for me. When you exercise your power to forgive someone, I think it affects them on a deeper realm than they realize. We hold people hostage when we choose not to forgive.

Instead, she declared, "It's over, it's done. The charges against you in my heart are dropped; they have been paid in full. You're free to go. There's no need to bring it up again in conversation, because I won't."

Instead of a paralyzing sentence being handed down, she lowered the gavel with a bang and said, "Case dismissed!" She lifted the enormous weight off my shoulders, and I'm free to move forward and be healed and made whole.

We all have that power in our possession, and when we choose to forgive a guilty person, we give that same gift of freedom. Please consider giving that gift to someone today. Life is too short to keep long ledgers. Erase the debt. It will be life changing for you both.

I've been a recipient of undeserved love and total forgiveness. God's amazing grace. God's riches at Christ's expense. Forgiveness of my sins. Forgiven by my wife and daughters, family and friends. Forgiveness glorifies God like nothing else I know. Forgiveness reveals God's love so clearly. We are never more like God than when we forgive, and we are never more unlike God than when we choose not to forgive.

It requires supernatural strength to forgive, others who have wronged us and don't deserve our forgiveness. Forgiveness sets people free, and it will set you free. I know this is true because I would still be bound, still be emotionally and mentally tortured regarding Cooper's death if not for God's forgiveness and my wife's forgiveness. Spiritual principles are at work here because the Bible says whatever we bind on earth will be bound in heaven, and whatever you loose on earth will be loosed in heaven. Please find it in your heart to forgive the person who has harmed you.

So, forgiveness is the key. Accept God's forgiveness, draw on His supernatural strength to forgive others, and forgive yourself. Then you will be that captive who is released and able to start down the path of grieving well.

Think about God's promise through Isaiah: "Come now, and let us reason together, saith the Lord: though your sins be as scarlet, they shall be as white as snow; though they be red like crimson, they shall be as wool" (Isaiah 1:18 KJV).

Consider it pure joy, my brothers, whenever you face
trials of many kinds, because you know that the testing
of your faith develops perseverance.

JAMES 1:2-3

14
Storms of Life

C. S. Lewis once wrote, "God whispers in our pleasure but shouts in our pain." Someone has suggested there are three phases of life. You are headed into a storm, currently in a storm, or coming out of a storm.

In the very familiar story about the wise and foolish builders, Jesus shared these words:

"Therefore everyone who hears these words of Mine and puts them into practice is like a wise man who built his house on the rock. The rain came down, the streams rose, and the winds blew and beat against that house; yet it did not fall, because it had its foundation on the rock. But everyone who hears these words of Mine and does not put them into practice is like a foolish man who built his house on sand. The rain came down, the streams rose, and the winds blew and beat against that house, and it fell with a great crash" (Matthew 7:24-27).

Two men. One man heard the words of the Lord and put them into practice. The other man heard the teachings of Jesus and did not put them into practice. Both heard, but the difference between them is that one was obedient, and the other wasn't. For both men the rain came down, the streams rose, and the winds blew and beat against their houses. You see, the storms of life are inevitable. Jesus said in another passage that it rains on the just and unjust alike. Contrary to some popular "name it and claim it" teaching, it is impossible to go from the cradle to the grave without some trials, temptations, and troubles.

When you read the Bible in context, you see that throughout Scripture men and women with great faith still endured hardships and suffering. In Job we read, "Yet man is born unto trouble, as the sparks fly upward" (Job 5:7). Heroes of the faith are described in the eleventh chapter of Hebrews, and look what they faced:

"Some faced jeers and flogging, while others were chained and put in prison. They were stoned; they were sawed in two; they were put to death by the sword. They went about in sheepskins and goatskins, destitute, persecuted, and mistreated – the world was not worthy of them. They wandered in deserts and mountains, and lived in caves and holes in the ground. These were all commended for their faith, yet none of them received what had been promised" (Hebrews 11:36-39).

Ecclesiastes reveals that this is the ebb and flow of life here on earth and "to everything there is a season."

Yes, there is that age-old unanswered question of why bad things happen to good people. It's a question that may remain a mystery this side of heaven. Consider that right now somewhere in the world there is a missionary who is absolutely in the center of God's will, but he and his family are being tortured for the cause of Christ. That doesn't seem fair and is hard to understand.

When I was a new believer I had friends imply that when you become a Christian you will no longer have any trouble. If you have enough faith your life will be problem free. That would be wonderful news if it were only true, but it's just not accurate. I believe in the promises of God along with His favor and blessings. He is all powerful and all knowing. Without a doubt He is a healer, and He performs miracles. But when you read the entire Bible you see that the storms of life affect everyone. We don't like to think about death and dying, but if you have elderly parents or grandparents, you will get that dreaded phone call. We don't dare dwell on it, but it's a bridge we will all cross if the Lord tarries.

If you need further proof that the storms of life are inevitable and that no one is exempt from suffering, consider the Apostle Paul. Here is someone God used to pen most of the New Testament, a man of great faith and close to the Lord by anyone's standards. Listen to his words:

> Are they servants of Christ? (I am out of my mind to talk like this.) I am more. I have worked much harder, been in prison more frequently, been flogged more severely, and been exposed to death again and again. Five times I received from the Jews the forty lashes minus one. Three times I was beaten with rods, once I was stoned, three times I was shipwrecked, I spent a night and a day in the open sea. I have been constantly on the move. I have been in danger from rivers, in danger from bandits, in danger from my own countrymen, in danger from Gentiles; in danger in the city, in danger in the country, in danger at sea, and in danger from false brothers. I have labored and toiled and have often gone without sleep; I have known hunger and thirst and have often gone without food; I have been cold and naked. Besides everything else, I face daily the pressure of my concern for all the churches (2 Corinthians 11:23-28).

So I'm convinced it is not a question of if, but when. Not if the storms of life will come, but when. No matter your gender, color, or age, the storms of life are inevitable. We are all candidates.

But there is good news! You can triumph over trouble. There is victory in the valley! Jesus said, in this world we will face trouble, but He has overcome the world. You can be an overcomer and there are lessons to be learned from the storm.

2008 was a difficult year for our family personally. Melanie's dad died of cancer, March 14, 2008. His death was devastating to say the least. Only one week after his death, Melanie had a miscarriage on Easter Sunday morning. Later that same year I had a near fatal horseback riding accident. The horseback ride resulted in me breaking my shoulder, five ribs, pelvis and tailbone, and bruising one lung. I also suffered from internal bleeding and additional injuries. I was hospitalized for 49 days, seven of which were in the intensive care unit. I made a full recovery from the horse wreck but was surprised that for many months the number one question I was asked was, "What did you do with the horse?"

I supposed after the horse had inflicted that much damage that I wouldn't be able to sell him, or even give him away. Would you believe, however, that two men were bidding against each other trying to buy that horse … they wanted to give it to their mother-in-law! Yes, I'm joking about the bidding war, but all of our trouble in 2008 was no laughing matter. Our consolation after an overwhelming amount of suffering was to think *At least the worst is behind us, and nothing could be worse than what we've experienced this year.* Little did we know that the following year we would face the greatest storm of our entire life, the death of our son, Cooper. Even considering all of the difficulties of the previous year, Cooper's death was worse than all the other things combined.

Many years ago I was traveling alone through Colorado. I was eating breakfast in a little cafe and had just bowed my head to return thanks for my food. When I looked up from saying the blessing, a distinguished military man sitting alone motioned for me to come over and join him. We quickly bonded as Christian brothers and enjoyed fellowship and good conversation. I confessed that I was at a crossroads in my life and at a low point. He instructed me to look out the window at Pike's Peak. He pointed to what he described as the timberline across the Rocky Mountains. It was a straight horizontal line where the vegetation grew up to the line, then stopped. Above the timberline it was craggy, rocky, and snow-capped. He further explained that trees and vegetation could not exist above the timberline because of the lack of oxygen and other factors.

He went on to explain, "Everyone enjoys a mountaintop experience, but there's no growth. The view is great. It's heady and exhilarating, but you can't live there. The air is too thin to sustain life. In the valley it's lush and green. Everyone wants to be on a mountaintop and no one wants to be in a deep valley. But the valley is where the most growth is." And if you think about the lesson I learned that day in Colorado Springs from that stranger, the hard times in our lives – the struggles, trials, and valleys – are when we are desperate and we turn to God for help.

In His Word God says if we draw near to Him, He will draw near to us. It's during the storms of life that we realize God is faithful, and we sense His presence. We can look back on our life and document the periods of greatest growth and see that the times when we were the closest to the Lord were most likely when we were at our lowest point. The first chapter of James tells us the trials of life teach us endurance. We see that this race was never meant to be easy. If it were, we would rely on ourselves and not trust the Lord or live in daily dependence on Him. Indeed, there are lessons to be learned in the storm, and during our terrible tragedy of losing Cooper we learned much. Here are just a few of the things we learned.

1. **Life is precious, but it's also fragile.** We learned how quickly life can completely change. We need not live in fear but strive to make every moment count because it's true what they say, "You never know when it's going to be your last opportunity to say 'I love you' to someone you care about." Make time for family and friends. Relish those moments together.

2. **Humility.** When something catastrophic happens, we realize how little we are in control of. God is big and we are small. There is a story told of a flea perched on an elephant's ear. The elephant walked across a wooden bridge. When they got to the other side the flea exclaimed, "Boy,

we sure made that bridge shake didn't we?" When you think about the big picture, it seems absurd for us to brag on our accomplishments, or even the times we think we are doing something big or important for God. We were completely humbled and overwhelmed by the death of our young son. Sometimes it takes something drastic to stop us in our tracks, help us prioritize and make a course correction. We were also genuinely humbled by the love and outpouring of support of others in our time of need.

3. The power of prayer. God hears and answers prayer. When we were too weak or depressed to pray for ourselves, we knew others were praying for us, and it was as if we could literally feel the prayers being offered up for us. Prayer is the difference maker.

4. The power of God's word. The Bible is the greatest book that has ever been written. It is the inerrant, infallible Word of God. It is God breathed. We talk to God through prayer, and God speaks to us through the Bible. There is no greater source for comfort, guidance, and wisdom. The greatest comfort we received while we were grieving was from personal Bible study, especially the Psalms.

5. The importance of the body of Christ. We saw the church in action. From small gestures of kindness to larger ones, every card, meal or thoughtful act made a difference and had an impact in our time of suffering.

6. The sovereignty of God. He is the potter, we are the clay. He is the shepherd, we are the sheep. God has a purpose and a plan. Even our darkest day did not catch Him by surprise. Lord, help us come to the place where we can pray "not my will but Thine be done."

7. Provision. God provided a sacrifice for Abraham on Mt. Moriah and ravens to feed Elijah by the brook. He provided a cruse of oil for the widow and an ark for Noah and his family. He promises to supply all your needs: "But my God shall supply all your needs according to His riches in glory by Christ Jesus" (Philippians 4:19 KJV). His grace is sufficient, and we discovered that even during a storm God is faithful. He will give you exactly what you need precisely when you need it.

8. Peace. "Do not be anxious about anything but in everything by prayer and petition, with thanksgiving, present your request to God. And the peace of God which passeth all understanding will guard your hearts and minds in Christ Jesus" (Philippians 4:6-7 KJV). Peace is not the absence of trouble, peace is the presence of God. Even in the middle of our suffering, we often sensed a sweet peace that transcended our understanding and can only be explained as coming from God. We experienced that paradox of having a perfect peace when all around us the storm was raging.

"Thou wilt keep him in perfect peace, whose mind is stayed on Thee: because he trusteth in Thee" (Isaiah 26:3 KJV).

9. Presence. We've experienced the faithful presence of God during our difficult journey. God led the Israelites with fire by night and a pillar of cloud by day. He has promised never to leave us or forsake us. He was with David in the lion's den. With Shadrach, Meshach and Abednego, He was the fourth man in the fire, and He will be there for you.

> Moses said to the Lord, "You have been telling me, 'Lead these people,' but You have not let me know whom You will send with me. You have said, 'I know you by name and you have found favor with Me.' If I have found favor in Your eyes, teach me Your ways so I may know You and continue to find favor with You. Remember that this nation is Your people."

> The Lord replied, "My Presence will go with you, and I will give you rest." Then Moses said to Him, "If Your Presence does not go with us, do not send us up from here" (Exodus 33:12-15).

10. This world is not our home. Trials, trouble, and tragedy have a way of reminding us that we are sojourners. We are just pilgrims passing through and heaven is our home and great reward. Tim Hall, a pastor friend from Kentucky, suggested after Cooper's death that we would never listen to a sermon or hear a song about heaven the same way ever again. He was right. Having a close loved one in heaven gives you fresh perspective about all things eternal. Consider these inspiring verses:

"I consider that our present sufferings are not worth comparing with the glory that will be revealed in us" (Romans 8:18).

"Therefore, we do not lose heart. Though outwardly we are wasting away, yet inwardly we are being renewed day by day. For our light and momentary troubles are achieving for us an eternal glory that far outweighs them all. So we fix our eyes not on what is seen, but on what is unseen. For what is seen is temporary, but what is unseen is eternal" (2 Corinthians 4:16-18).

If we place our trust in Christ, we have assurance from the Bible that heaven will be our home. One day we will be safely home rejoicing in the promises we have in Revelation 21:4: "And God shall wipe away all tears from their eyes; and there shall be no more death, neither sorrow, nor crying; neither shall there be any more pain: for the former things are passed away."

For this reason I remind you to fan into flame the gift of God, which is in you through the laying on of my hands.

2 TIMOTHY 1:6

15

Flame On

Several months after Cooper's death we were approached by the leadership of American Family Association. "We noticed after this horrific event, you and Melanie haven't turned to drugs or alcohol or anything like that. You are still attending church and your marriage is intact," they said.

The death of a child puts a terrible strain on a marriage. The percentage of marriages that fail after the death of a child is extremely high. Just the sheer magnitude of the grief and pain that comes from losing a child can overwhelm a relationship. People who have lost a spouse or a parent as well as having a child die tell us there is no comparison. Losing a child is immeasurably more painful. After both of my parents died in 2011 I'm among the ranks that will tell you the same thing.

The leaders of AFA explained that they were thanking God for how well we seemed to be coping, fully acknowledging that it was because of God's great mercy and grace working in our life. We think that was evident to many people because, let's face it, you can't make it through such a tragedy in your own strength. It requires supernatural help from above.

AFA leadership explained that after watching our example, they realized how few resources there are for families who had a child die. They wanted to make a documentary telling our story to offer hope on the other side of tragedy. The movie would not be sold but actually given away as a free resource to help hurting people heal.

It had only been a few months since Cooper's death, so they were very cautious and extremely sensitive. We were asked to pray about it and if (and only if) we felt we could talk about it on camera, then they were open to pursue this project. I want to be very clear about how gingerly this was handled. They were sensitive to how raw our emotions were so soon after Cooper's death. They reiterated that this DVD would not be sold but given away as a means to help those who are grieving.

We did have some family members who felt it was insensitive to be approached so soon about making this documentary, and that's understandable. Melanie and I wrestled with it, too.

I was open to the idea, however, because I've known the leaders of AFA for a long time. I am thankful for Don Wildmon, Tim Wildmon, and the entire Wildmon family for their faithfulness in leading American Family Association, a ministry that is dedicated to turning our nation back to its Judeo-Christian roots and to helping hurting people. This family and this ministry have been a tremendous blessing to our family and the entire nation. When Don Wildmon began American Family Association in 1977, his desire was to have an impact on our culture for the cause of Christ.[6] I know the hearts and motives of the Wildmon family – and I trust them.

So I considered their idea about a documentary. The movie-makers explained that by making the film sooner rather than later, they were hoping to capture the grieving process in real time. Usually when you watch a similar documentary it's the telling of a story 10 years later and seems to be sanitized. It fails to portray the raw, gut level emotion because so many years have passed. AFA's movie-makers weren't trying to exploit us but rather trying to be so authentic that it would connect with those who would relate and are so desperate for answers. They were trying to do something that hadn't been done in order to provide maximum ministry. It would be an emotional tightrope, but the film would be so much more powerful because of that very emotion.

We prayed about our involvement in the movie. Originally, Melanie, wasn't completely on board. She is a private person whereas I'm more public. And realistically, we knew the emotional cost might be too high a price for us to pay. But after much prayer we felt that the good that would come from the project would outweigh the pain it would require to tell our story. Throughout our entire journey of grieving, 2 Corinthians 1:4 became a very personal and profound motivation. That verse speaks of God comforting us in our affliction so we can comfort others when they are afflicted. This became our motivation for agreeing to do the film, too.

As the filming began we were constantly asked how we were holding up and reminded that if it was too much to bear, they would immediately pull the plug on the whole project. The emotional drain of filming actually did take its toll and we stopped for many months. We finally felt strong enough to continue and filming resumed. With many prayers being offered for our family and the entire project, we finally finished the documentary we would name **Flame On**. "Flame on," was an expression from one of Cooper's favorite super heroes – the Human Torch. For Cooper, "Flame on!" meant "Go faster!" With lots of time to think and reflect on every detail of the accident, I realized that "Flame on" were the last two words that Cooper said before he passed from this world to the next.

Kendra White, a writer-director for American Family Studios, was assigned to take the lead on the project. Almost everyone at AFA/AFR knew Cooper and loved him. Interestingly, Kendra was newly hired and had never met him. I wondered how someone can tell the story of our precious son when they never met him and certainly didn't know him. Our concerns were quickly put to rest after several interviews with Kendra. She is a talented young lady who is a spirit-filled Christian and head over heels in love with Jesus. She has impeccable character and integrity. Her work ethic and her desire for excellence are inspiring.

Kendra asked us if we had any home movies and if we would be willing to allow those in the film. This was amusing to us because Melanie would occasionally give me a hard time for dragging out the camcorder to record every moment of our children's lives. She would sigh and say, "You and that camcorder." Can you imagine how many times we have rejoiced knowing that we captured so much video of our little boy who we'll never see again until our reunion in heaven? Of course, we had no idea that our personal home movies would be watched by hundreds of thousands of people either. No reenactors here. The family you see portrayed is actually us. In fact, the home movies easily told such an authentic story that they make up a large portion of the documentary.

I always encourage people to video their family and take lots of pictures. No one ever regretted having movies and photos of loved ones. Holidays, vacations, birthdays, graduations … You can't turn back time and relive those priceless moments, but you almost can if you caught it on video. No one will regret taping their sweet children's laughter and the voices of loved ones. Photos are nice, but video includes sound. How amazing would it be for us to be able to watch and actually hear the voices and accents of our ancestors from days long gone? We can give that gift to our children and children's children by filming them. Our kids grow up so quickly and they change so much. Record those memories!

Kendra was amazing to watch as she orchestrated all the elements and decided the direction of **Flame On**. We were allowed to include key players in our story and some others were suggested and included. Unfortunately, not all of our loved ones and those significant to the story got included, mostly due to time constrains. How do you share someone's entire life story in only forty-two minutes?

For those of you who have seen the film, you might have noticed that everyone who was interviewed seemed to stay on the same basic script with certain Biblical themes – like the sovereignty of God. Many of those featured in **Flame On** quoted the same Bible verses and offered the exact same counsel but from different perspectives. It was almost as if instruction sheets with bullet points were passed out and everyone was encouraged to stay with those guidelines. But the fact was that no one saw any of the footage from the others. When everyone was taped they just sat down and shared from their hearts. And everyone said the same thing! Only Steve and Annie Chapman and Dr. James Dobson saw portions of the raw edit because they were included in the bonus features. No one else in the film saw a single minute of the contributions from the others. The Holy Spirit seemed to speak through each one with such unity, and everyone's part seemed just to flow in concert offering help and hope to those who are hurting. The entire project was bathed in prayer, and I'm convinced it was anointed by God to be life changing.

Here's how Kendra explains her experiences working on **Flame On**:

I remember that interview like it was yesterday. We hooked up the microphones, got the tissues on stand by, and sat the Jaspers down on a brown couch in their cozy home. Then came the hard part. For over two hours, I probed the depths of their hearts and listened to their brutally honest, most intimate answers. I still have no idea how I made it through that interview without falling apart. All I can say is this: The Lord gave each of us a ridiculous amount of strength that day. He guided our conversation and His presence was very obvious in that room!

Next, I began interviewing friends and family members. Every single person I talked to raved about Cooper, the little bubble of joy who loved dressing up as super heroes and singing at the top of his lungs. So many stories! So much love! I knew that in order for the audience to really feel the Jaspers' loss, they had to get to know the little blonde-headed treasure that had captured the hearts of so many. That's when God gave me the idea of using the Jaspers' home video footage.

As the story progressed, it was unreal how many of the memories that were shared in the interviews were also captured on tape! It was an editor's dream! As I watched through hours of silly family get-togethers, I fell in love with the entire family. I could tell that they were the real deal. Their love for each other and their walks with the Lord shined through every birthday party, school play, and sporting event.

But then came the hard part. I'd edited the "get to know the family" section of the documentary and had even covered Cooper's accident. But once I hit the part where the Jaspers had to pick up the pieces and deal with their grief…it became unbearable to edit. I remember one day the heaviness set in, and I had to get up from my computer and walk away. I went into a side room at AFA, closed the door, and got on my face before the Lord. I sensed so strongly that the Lord was creating something powerful that would be used to bring hope to the hopeless. All I could do was seek the Lord's guidance on how to handle such a powerful story.

After much prayer, I cautiously approached the next stage of editing. One thing I just couldn't seem to get out of my head was that statement J.J. made right after he found out Cooper had passed. He said, "The Lord giveth and the Lord taketh away. Blessed be the name of the Lord." Who does that? Who loses a child and then says that?

I quickly learned that the quotation was from the book of Job. So I turned to Scripture and started reading. Then I began sorting through interviews and soon found that nearly every person we talked to quoted at least one passage from Job. Themes from the interviews began to come together as if everyone had scripted out exactly what they were going to say!

And then I came to the footage where J.J. began to preach the gospel message straight to the hearts of those listening. He said that Jesus was the only way he and his family made it through this, and he proceeded to lay out the plan of salvation in one of the most straightforward and powerful ways I think I've ever heard. I literally had goose bumps just watching it. To hear God's word spoken with such authority and from such genuine hearts was astounding.

There are some projects you are proud to be a part of, and then there are others that change you. Being a part of **Flame On** has truly changed me. Quotes from the movie often come to my mind challenging me to press into Christ and to make every moment count. God is so glorified in this story! Thank you, J.J. and Melanie, for being willing to be used by Him in such a powerful way!

Thank you again, Kendra, for your willingness to be used by God to produce and direct such a Christ-centered project for the glory of God.

When we began filming, Melanie agreed to sit beside me during the interviews and hold my hand while silently praying, but she informed me she would not talk. She said she would only nod her head. Melanie is not at all comfortable on stage or in the spotlight. She is generally shy and has no desire to be in front of a microphone or camera. Many people experience what's known as "mic(rophone) fright," and most of you can appreciate the fact that she is terrified to speak in front of a crowd. However, as someone once said, if you want to make God laugh, tell him your plans or tell Him what you'll never do! And it was true in our case: Melanie had her plans, and God had His. Those of you who have seen the film know that some of the most powerful moments in **Flame On** are when Melanie shared from a mother's heart. Trust me when I tell you it was the Holy Spirit speaking through Melanie. Moreover, since the debut of **Flame On,** Melanie has been invited to speak at a half dozen women's conferences and Bible studies. The one who vowed to never be a speaker is doing an absolutely amazing job. Thank you, Melanie, for your willingness to obey God even with the noticeable heel marks where God had to drag you. Moses knows just how you feel!

Immediately after **Flame On** was finished and distributed, it was well received. Over 50,000 copies have been given away and well over

100,000 people have watched it online at www.flameon.net. We are humbled and amazed by how fruitful the film has been to inspire others and offer hope in the Lord. We have heard from hundreds of pastors who have shown it on Wednesday or Sunday nights at their church services. In fact, AFA made the film 42 minutes long for that very reason. A pastor could introduce it, show the movie, then offer concluding thoughts, challenges, an altar call or make appropriate remarks considering the audience and do so in one hour.

God has blessed **Flame On** in numerous other ways. For example, it was shown on a television station in South Korea that aired across the entire nation in November 2013. It was nominated for an award at the 2012 San Antonio Independent Christian Film Festival and was a semi-finalist in the documentary category. Our entire family was invited and we were all privileged to fly to Texas as representatives for **Flame On**. Only the Lord knows how far reaching **Flame On** will be. We heard from a pastor who showed the film to his congregation in Birmingham, England. AY-TV in India asked permission to dub it in their language and show it in Asia. Melanie received a text from a friend on vacation in the Caribbean. Her friend was in the hotel room flipping through the channels and **Flame On** was on TV in Jamaica! It appears the Lord is allowing the film to ricochet around the globe all for the glory of God!

Best-selling author and pastor Max Lucado saw the film and I was invited to join him and Shelia Walsh for a radio special. After we taped the program, it aired on many stations nationwide. Max reached out to us again asking permission to share our story in a sermon at his church complete with Cooper's picture displayed on the big screen overhead. When I think of Max Lucado telling the story of our little Cooper, it's amazing and humbling indeed. Next, Max asked permission to include our story in his book, *You'll Get Through This.*

Yes, God is using this story for His glory, and we believe His promise that He is able to do exceeding, abundantly more than we could ask or imagine. The testimonies from those who have watched it have a common theme, that God used the film to help them turn a corner or get over a hump in their struggles. Many said the movie actually helped them start the grieving process.

One such story is about a counselor who was working with a woman distressed over loss of family. Her son, daughter-in-law, and their children were all brutally murdered. Can you even imagine? The grandchildren had been temporarily living with the grandmother and had become more like her own children which even compounded the horrific loss. The counselor said that he had used textbook techniques to try to help this grandmother but to no avail. She could not move forward. He said that after many months she had not budged one inch from her paralyzed state of grief, depression, bitterness, and unforgiveness. The counselor had exhausted all his tools and expertise as a licensed professional. Finally, out of exasperation, at another counseling session where she was unable to gain any traction at all, he asked her permission to show the film. He explained it was a last ditch effort on his part because nothing was working. They watched **Flame On**. She had a complete breakthrough and made so much progress that she insisted he contact us at AFA headquarters and personally thank me and my family on her behalf.

I was speaking in Philadelphia, Mississippi, and arrived at the meeting very early. As I arrived the only couple who were there quickly approached me. While they were only a few feet away the woman collapsed in my arms and started sobbing. After she regained her composure, they both explained that their son had died in an accident only a month earlier. As they were expressing gratitude for the help they received from watching **Flame On**, I remembered the original intent of the filmmakers to capture grief in real time to relate with others on the deepest level. Some critics of **Flame On** asked why would we want to offer a resource to struggling people that is only going to make them cry more? With that in mind, I posed this question to this sweet couple: "Since you are so freshly grieving, why would you watch **Flame On** so soon?

I wish everyone responsible for the film could have been there to hear their response. They said, "We had so many questions and were so desperate for answers, when someone gave us the DVD we watched it immediately. Two minutes into the movie we knew you were genuine and you had been there. It was real, the emotion was so raw and as we heard you tell your story, we were clinging to every word because we immediately trusted what you had to say. We thought, *This family has been there. Whatever they say is what we need to hear.* We were at the lowest point of our lives, more desperate than we had ever been, and God used **Flame On** to give us hope." They continued sharing how the film was a faith builder, answered many questions, and helped them begin to grieve well.

I could fill the pages of an entire book with testimonies from people who have contacted us to share how the film impacted their lives. If you add up emails, phone calls, cards, etc., we have now heard from thousands who have benefited. Here is a sample of responses that were taken from the comment section on www.flameon.net:

Inspirational story of tragedy replaced with hope! – Cheryl

This story was absolutely amazing and so heartfelt. I look to God more now than I ever have. – April

This video can be a tremendous instrument to those suffering from the loss of a loved one, especially that of a parent losing a child. Praise God for the Jaspers' willingness to share their story and be so very transparent during such a painful time to help others. Tears burst from my eyes as I saw the miracle added to your family a year later and to witness your trust in His sovereignty. – Lesa

I am so sorry that I heard this story, and yet at the same time overwhelm-

ingly grateful that I heard this story. – Bobby

Losing a child terrifies me, as it does any parent. But your story has given me a foundation to stand on to face the coming storms of life. Thank you for using Cooper's beautiful life to share your faith. May God continue to give you peace daily that you will see your sweet boy again someday, and will have a chance to make up for lost time. God bless you all. – Becky

I watched this video for the third time tonight, and once again it has left me with the desire to know God more. After 57 years of belonging to the Catholic Faith which I love, I don't believe any sermon or testimony has touched my heart like this story. Seeing true and authentic trust and love for God through your eyes in the midst of something so so tragic as losing little Cooper gives me such hope and a more steadfast love for God. I pray for God's grace to continue to shower down on your family always. – Charlotte

Thank you, American Family Association! And thank you, Jesus. You turn tragedy into triumph and bring beauty from ashes.

Therefore encourage one another and build each other up, just as in fact you are doing.
THESSALONIANS 5:11

16

Encouragement from Unexpected Sources

The letter I received from the sweet lady, a listener, from Arkansas, explained that her sibling had died in an accident when she was a young girl. It affected her parents so dramatically that they refused to let her (the surviving sister) learn to ride a bike, roller-skate or take any risk at all. She explained that she wasn't allowed to learn to swim – in fact, she was forbidden to get in any body of water above her ankles. She lived a sheltered life isolated from what would be considered normal, fun, youthful activities because of her overprotective parents' unnatural fears. She lamented about how much she missed out on and confessed that she was emotionally scarred due to her childhood and was not well adjusted socially.

In her letter filled with compassion she expressed that she knew we were just experiencing a wonderful father-and-son time together and an accident happened. She offered such loving, earnest condolences and she concluded her letter by saying, "I would've given anything to have taken a ride in a dune buggy with my daddy, even if it had killed me."

Steven Curtis Chapman is one of my all-time favorite Christian singers. As a singer/songwriter he has garnered nearly all of the music awards available. Beyond his incredible talent as a writer and singer, I've always been impressed by his integrity and character. He has been an excellent role model for those who listen to his songs on the radio or attend his concerts. Steven Curtis is a dedicated Christian and committed family man.

The Christian community was shocked when Steven Curtis Chapman and his wife, Mary Beth, experienced the unthinkable: In May 2008 their beautiful, sweet five-year-old daughter, Maria, was killed in an automobile accident. We repeatedly asked our listeners to pray for this precious family after hearing about this horrible event. Even after months passed we reminded our listeners to continue to pray for the Chapmans as they continued to grieve. I was devastated for the entire family but particularly for their son, Will Franklin, who was driving the vehicle involved in the accident. My heart was heavy for him. Privately in conversations with Melanie, I said, even with the Lord's help, how do you ever get over it when you were the one driving? How can you cope the rest of your life with the guilt, regret, and all the "what-ifs" that would surely follow? Little did I know that one year later I would be in a similar situation as the one who was doing the driving when Cooper died.

The Chapmans' story is well documented in Mary Beth's inspiring book, *Choosing to See.* With the world watching, the Chapman family weathered the storm, gave glory to God, and was an inspiration to many, including our family.

Immediately after our accident we were surprised to get an email from Steven Curtis who was on a trip to China. As soon as he received word about Cooper's death he wrote:

Dear J. J. and Melanie,

I received a call from my mom this morning (I'm in China with my family right now.) telling me the tragic news of your loss of your son, Cooper. All I know to say are the words that somehow were the most comforting to me in the terrible dark "valley of the shadow of death" that you both are walking through right now. There are no words. There are no words sufficient for this pain, this mystery, this loss. I'm just so very, very sorry. I weep with you and I trust and believe that our Savior weeps with you.

And as Greg Laurie reminded me after we lost Maria but before he lost his own son, our future with Maria and Cooper is so much greater than our past! May this truth and this hope help you simply breathe in the hours and days ahead.

There is a lot more I could be tempted to say right now to try to encourage, but at this moment I'll just say again, I'm so sorry. If there's an appropriate time for us to speak on the phone or even face to face in the coming days, I'd consider it a privilege to grieve with you.

With Hope,
Steven Curtis

Wise, compassionate words from someone who has "been there." God knows exactly where you are and what you need, when you need it. He can nudge a famous singer's heart to respond from halfway around the world to offer encouragement from an unexpected source! It was a blessing to receive a personal note from someone so busy. In fact *every* phone call, email, card and letter from concerned people blessed us and encouraged us beyond words. It helped us grieve well.

Initially after Cooper's death, the overwhelming grief came wave after wave, knocking us over emotionally, spiritually and physically. It seemed there would be no relief from the intensity of the hurt, loss and heartache. When we finally caught a break between waves and seemed to catch a quick breath, another reality hit us right between the eyes. Funeral home bills! Anyone who has lost a loved one knows that the cost associated with the funeral services, the cemetery plot, headstone, etc. is staggering. If your loved one lingers with an illness, you face almost insurmountable hospital and doctor bills. Even if you live within a budget, you really never imagine that your child will die – and thus don't prepare for it. Unfortunately financial difficulty is added to the list of emotional, physical, and spiritual despair.

I love small town life. In a small town your banker can also be your friend. That was the case with Lisa, the branch manager of the local bank where we are customers.

Lisa called excited to share something that had just happened at the bank. A teller was out and Lisa "just happened" to be working in the teller's place. A couple approached her and asked, "Is this the place where the Jaspers do their banking?" Naturally, Lisa explained that according to bank policy she couldn't divulge information about customers' accounts.

The couple went on to explain that they were from Tennessee and were regular American Family Radio listeners. They had contacted American Family Radio to ask where we did our banking, and they thought it was this bank branch. The couple continued to say that they followed our story, were saddened, and then rightly assumed we would not have anticipated paying for the funeral for one of our children. The couple expressed how they felt prompted from the Lord to deposit money in our account.

Lisa made an exception to allow it and then proceeded to tell the couple that she knew us personally and asked if they would mind if she called so we could meet them and thank them. They were modest and humble, and wished to remain anonymous. Lisa pleaded with them saying, "This will drive them crazy, not knowing whom to thank." The couple was firm in their position wanting God to get all the glory. They were so serious about their anonymity they had already secured a cashier's check with no name on it and no way to trace it.

After Lisa exhausted all efforts to find out their identity, she acted as our liaison and on behalf of our family patiently shared with this sweet couple how special Cooper was and how we were an authentic Christian family. She continued to tell them that we did not have the money for the funeral bills and offered gratitude on our behalf.

It was no accident that our friend Lisa "just happened" to be working at that exact teller window precisely when the mystery couple made their trip from Tennessee to Mississippi to be such a blessing in our lives. I hesitate even sharing this story because it's so personal and we have all been taught it's not good manners to discuss finances publicly. But we wanted to share this because all the glory belongs to the One who promises to help us according to His riches in glory. I have heard marvelous testimonies like this from others over the years in dynamic church services, but it always seemed to happen to someone else. This time it happened to us.

We may never meet the kind, humble, generous couple who helped us. Lisa described them as appearing of modest means, and they did not have an air about them. They did not appear wealthy, which makes the story more remarkable when you consider the sacrifice involved.

Dear generous couple from somewhere in Tennessee:

If you just happen to be reading this book, maybe this is our only chance to say thank you. Thank you for loving our family and demonstrating such grace and compassion. We have prayed that God would reward you and bless you for your amazing kindness. Please know that Almighty God used you to help our family in a miraculous way at the lowest point in our lives. You'll never know how humbled and unworthy we felt when you traveled to Tupelo, Mississippi, and deposited money into our account. The amount paid for the funeral bills almost to the penny.

Glory to God! Hallelujah, Jehovah Jireh! Thank you, Jesus, for en-couragement from unexpected sources!

Jesus wept.
JOHN 11:35

17

Grieving Well

Several years after our parents died, my sister, Kelly, posted this on social media:

My heart has been very heavy lately regarding loss. It seems like every time I turn around, someone I know has lost a loved one. I understand the pain of losing someone you love. I don't think I've given myself the opportunity to grieve the loss of my parents, so that is the reason for this post. This is not a pity party. I'm just sharing my heart.

1 Thessalonians 4:13-18 says, "Brothers and sisters, we do not want you to be uninformed about those who sleep in death, so that you do not grieve like the rest of mankind, who have no hope. For we believe that Jesus died and rose again, and so we believe that God will bring with Jesus those who have fallen asleep in Him."

The Scripture tells us not to grieve as those "who have no hope," but it doesn't tell us not to grieve. Losing a loved one is a very real loss. Your life is forever altered. There is a void, a seat missing at the table, and that person is no longer on the other end of the phone. The conversations are gone, and there are no more hugs or laughter. There is just a memory. At my nephew's funeral, the pastor said a death is like an amputation. You are forever aware of the loss, but eventually you learn to live life without that person. God is a God of comfort, and He will carry us and comfort us and give us peace, but He also created us with emotions. When Lazarus died, Jesus was deeply moved at their sorrow

(John 11:33). It is okay to grieve. There is no blueprint or time line for grief. It is a process. There are so many Scriptures about God's comfort and peace, and I will continue to hold fast to them as I grieve. But I will grieve. And for those who think too much time has passed, or wonder why I still mourn, please keep your opinions to yourself. I am taking the time I need for me. God created me uniquely, and He alone knows what my heart needs and how to heal it. If you have lost a loved one and are reading this, I pray that you let the God who created you and knows you, comfort you and heal your heart in His time.

Kelly's heartfelt words come from someone who realizes that grieving is necessary. Grieving is Biblical. But grieving is also brutal.

This was evident to us as the "firsts" began to come. We were warned the first Thanksgiving, the first Christmas and the first birthday without Cooper would be nearly unbearable, and we knew to brace ourselves for those. But we weren't prepared for the common everyday "firsts" – the first trip to the grocery store without him, the first church service or dining out at a restaurant with the painfully obvious empty chair. We got hammered emotionally by the first everything. What made the grieving process so difficult for us was how often we were ambushed by grief. We could be having a fairly normal day, and without warning there would be a familiar smell or a song we associated with Cooper and we were immediately reduced to shoulder-shaking sobs. It didn't matter where we were, we couldn't control it.

During the first few days and weeks after Cooper's death, Melanie and I spent a lot of time sobbing uncontrollably and holding each other close. Between sobs we would pray a simple prayer, "Lord, help us grieve well." We weren't even sure what that meant or what it looked like, but oftentimes we felt we were just hanging on by a thread.

PRINCIPLES FOR GRIEVING

The subtitle for this book is Finding Hope to Grieve Well, because that was our prayer repeatedly in the early days and we believe God answered that prayer. This chapter includes helpful, practical tips in hopes that you can grieve well. Please keep in mind this is not a comprehensive manual on how to grieve. Here are a few of the barest and broadest of principles we learned in this painful process:

There is a commonality to human suffering and grieving. For those who have walked the path of sorrow and grief, there are things we all share to some degree.

In his March 2010 *AFA Journal* article titled, "Grieving Well," AFA editor Randall Murphree says, "Whether it's the death of an aging parent who has suffered for a long season, or the sudden accidental death of a young child, grief has a way of putting us all on common ground."

Much scientific research indicates that there is a pattern to grieving – certain stages through which all who mourn go.

In *Waiting for Answers – A Parent's Guide to Grief, Resolution and Healing*, Betsy Haid cites research and identifies these stages:

> … the first stage of grief [is] denial, where grieving individuals simply cannot believe they've lost a loved one or that death is imminent. They aren't able to accept that this tragedy has happened to them.
>
> The next phase of grief … is anger. In this phase bereaved parents or others accept that the loss is real, but they feel a sense of rage at the unfairness of the death.
>
> Following anger is the stage of grief known as bargaining, when parents try to strike a deal emotionally with nature, the universe, or God. Even though they realize intellectually that nothing can bring their child back to life, parents in this phase are often praying for God to turn back the clock or to take their lives instead of the child's; or they may promise to make

significant changes in their lives if God will restore the child.

After a time, bargaining gives way to depression. In this stage of grief, people fully realize the inevitability of the loss and their inability to change it. Feelings of guilt and helplessness mark this phase, and many people will withdraw from friends and family in order to find the emotional and psychological energy to process the finality of losing a son or daughter.

At last, bereaved parents will enter the final stage of grief, acceptance, where they reengage in work and relationships and begin to plan for the future, acknowledging that their child will not be a part of that future except in their memories.[7]

The grieving process is intensely personal and often unique. While all who mourn may share many things, this does not imply that we all suffer through grief in exactly the same way. Haid says, "The stages of grief apply to all of us, but reactions within the stages of grief are unique to each individual."

How could it be otherwise? We have different personalities and we don't all respond the same. Melanie and I learned that everyone grieves differently and on his or her own timetable.

As Murphree so aptly put it, "Everyone who has lost a loved one has his own unique journey through the valley."

I was impressed by a simple post I read on Facebook regarding the uniqueness of that journey: "No rule book. No time frame. No judgment. Grief is as individual as a fingerprint."

Please take as long as you need and grieve in a way that is appropriate for you as long as you are not harming yourself or others.

Great loss will expose both your strengths and your weaknesses. You are what you are when tragedy strikes. All it reveals is what your life has been built upon to that point.

How will each man's life fare when the storms of life strike him? It depends what his life has been built upon.

Melanie and I, along with author and pastor Richard Exley were interviewed for the *AFA Journal* article mentioned earlier. In the interview Pastor Exley said, "Experience has shown that most people grieve the same way they live. If you have lived a life of faith, one grounded in the Word of God, and you have surrounded yourself with a network of family and friends you will be prepared for whatever loss you suffer. This will not eliminate the pain but will give you the strength to transcend it."

Stick with the basics. Walking through the valley of great sorrow doesn't require anything profound – you just have to put one foot in front of the other.

There wasn't a magic bullet or a secret formula when Melanie and I were grieving. It was just going back to the basics, going to the root of what every believer knows will keep you on course or will help you keep your sanity. You get up, you read your Bible whether you feel like it or not, you pray even when you don't want to, and you stay connected to a community of believers. Those were the lifelines for us.

Don't let anger turn to bitterness. Emotional responses to great loss are normal, but we can't allow those emotions to destroy us.

"Anger is almost always part of the grieving process, especially when a loved one dies prematurely," said Exley. "If the grieving person can tell God how he is really feeling, especially the feelings he thinks a Christian shouldn't have, he is well on his way to moving from anger to acceptance."

"Anger turns to bitterness when we bottle it up," he added. "It may be helpful to remember that God can only heal the things we give Him. Anything we deny or repress is beyond the reach of His healing grace. Also we need to remember that moving from anger to acceptance is often a process rather than a single event. We will need to confess our angry feelings to the Lord each time we experience them and give Him permission to change the way we feel."

We've spoken with many parents who have lost children, and anger and bitterness is a major struggle. Our biggest challenge was depression. We felt like we were staying only one step ahead of being completely paralyzed by it. The first year was the most difficult for me personally, and then there was an occasional break in the dark clouds, allowing some sunshine to enter, followed by less frequent periods of deep sadness. It seems that although time didn't heal, it helped. For Melanie, the second year was actually worse than the first.

Like everything else in our lives, we must give our experiences – and our thoughts and feelings about them – to God. Only He can use them to shape us into His image.

Exley said: "How grief changes a person depends on how he responds to it. If the grieving person blames God and becomes trapped in anger and bitterness he will likely become a prematurely old and bitter person. On the other hand, if one turns to God in the hour of grief, God will redeem sorrow by giving him not only comfort, but also an enlarged capacity for compassion and a new empathy for others."

Allow friends near. When we are mourning, often we are tempted to isolate ourselves. But that will cut us off from the grace that God wants to impart through our loved ones.

"I tend to push people away when I'm depressed," Melanie told *AFA Journal.* "I just want to be by myself. I think one of the best things that we did was allow our friends and church family to come in and be there for us. They don't have to say anything. Just knowing that they are there is such a comfort."

Know that you will recover. It's difficult to believe that when you are in the midst of the worst anguish you've ever experienced, but it's true.

"I often describe the experience by comparing grief to the ocean tides," Exley explained. "Immediately following the death of a loved one, the tide of grief comes rushing in like a storm surge and it stays for a long time. When you're grieving, you often feel like you are drowning. Slowly the tide goes out and you relax a little, but before you've had time to draw a deep breath, the tide of grief comes rolling back in. This goes on for many months, often for as long as two or three years.

"Over the course of time you will notice that the tide of grief does not come in quite as far, nor does it stay in nearly as long. Little by little you realize that you are having more good days than bad days; that the tide of grief is going further out and staying out longer."

Seek a qualified counselor. A pastor or mature Christian friend is a good place to start, but grief this severe may require a licensed professional. We recommend using a Bible-based Christian counselor for the best results.

Be very careful with pharmaceuticals. In our experience I was surprised how many people were quick to offer us medications and actually insist on prescribing them. We chose not to go that route. While we certainly don't judge those who do use medicines properly, we were cautioned by some who had gotten addicted to prescription drugs during their grieving. Others told us that their dependence on medications only served to temporarily mask the pain. Instead of helping, it only prolonged it, and they found themselves several years down the road – after coming out of a drug-induced fog – having to start again from the beginning on their grieving journey.

Stay busy by serving others. It helps take your mind off your troubles.

Prepare for the day when friends and family must leave. We were warned that our grief would really intensify at around the 30-day mark after friends and family returned to their normal life and schedule. It was true.

Try to have a ready answer. One thing we weren't prepared for was how to answer questions about the number of our children or how to explain our story. Because our living children now consist of all girls, when we meet new people someone will almost always remark, "Oh, you don't have any boys?" or something similar. Each time we answer them honestly it's always very awkward for them. If we avoid answering or quickly change the subject then we feel guilty and feel like we didn't honor the memory of our sweet son. We never want to appear rude or make people feel uncomfortable, and we have answered in a variety of ways. But to be honest we still don't have a solution to this dilemma. Just be prepared for this and have an answer that is best for your situation.

Trust God completely. He is the only one capable of sustaining you during tragedy. When we were in the middle of our darkest times, Melanie and I would sometimes hold each other between sobs and say, "How does anyone go through this without God? Without the Word of God? Without the people of God?"

Emotionally, we finally hit bottom. And there we found the good news – the bottom is rock solid. The bottom is the Lord Jesus Christ and His Word. His promises are true. His grace is sufficient. He gives a peace that surpasses all our understanding.

Much of this came through people. Because of the body of Christ, God's mercy and grace have been amplified in our lives through this experience. The Lord has given us strength to make it. And if He helps us, He can help you, too.

We don't expect to ever get over the grief, but with God's help, we'll get through it.

PRINCIPLES FOR FRIENDS WHO WANT TO COMFORT THOSE WHO ARE GRIEVING

During this process of grieving, we also discovered some principles that will better prepare us to comfort others in their grief. Here are some of the things we suggest you consider when you desire to minister to your grieving friends:

When you have opportunity to comfort a grieving friend, less is more. Resist the temptation to lecture or preach to a suffering friend, and don't attempt to explain the tragedy in a manner that denies the sorrow of a grief-stricken person.

"Usually the less we say the better," suggests Exley. "Our presence is much more powerful than anything we can say. Just being there is the most helpful thing we can offer. An arm around the shoulders, a squeeze of the hand, is what the grieving person needs most, especially early on.

"Remember, there are no words that can restore the departed person to life. Neither are there any words that can take away the pain death has caused, so don't try to fix things. You can't. Just weep with those who weep."

Melanie said, "So many people say things to try and encourage you. They mean well, but boy, sometimes it just doesn't come out right. I guess the best thing to say is, 'I don't know what to say,' or, 'I'll be praying for you.' Or just be quiet and just be there for those who are grieving."

What should you say about God? Surely we should encourage our suffering friend in some manner though, right? Absolutely! But there are only a few things a grieving person wants to hear in a time of unspeakable loss.

"Even when grieving people ask questions it is usually not answers they are seeking but assurance," Exley said. "Intuitively they know there are no answers, but they want to be assured of at least three things: (1) that God cares, that He is suffering with them; (2) that God is near, that He will never forsake them; and (3) that God will redeem their tragedy, that He will not allow their suffering to be wasted."

Nevertheless, we learned that saying something to a grieving person can still be very helpful. We got thousands of emails from AFR listeners within a matter of a few days after Cooper died. Every single night, we sat around our kitchen table and we read, out loud, the cards and emails from our listeners. We would just weep and read, but it helped us immensely.

Don't tell grieving friends that you know how they feel. You don't. Even if you've experienced a similar loss, human emotions are very fragile and very personal things.

Exley said, "Don't talk about a loss you have suffered as a way of trying to identify with the grieving person. Doing so serves only to trivialize his grief. Don't say, 'I know what you are feeling' You don't know what he is feeling. You may have suffered a similar loss but that doesn't mean you know what he is feeling.

Don't underestimate the comfort of practical helps during the grieving process. When you're suffering, it's hard to think about doing the everyday tasks that keep life moving along. So friends who can help with such matters are a true blessing.

Exley said, "On a practical level we should offer to take care of some of the mundane details of daily life – offer to pick up the laundry or bring a meal. Run whatever errands need running or drive the kids wherever they need to go.

One perfect example of the small things we appreciated was when people sent photos of their own kids in which Cooper also appeared. After all, when he died, we knew we would never be able to take another photo of him. These were new pictures to us, and they were worth more than gold.

Resources for grieving

We discovered numerous resources for those who are grieving the loss of a loved one. Here are some we recommend:

Facing Death and the Life After by Billy Graham

When You Lose A Loved One by Charles Allen

Confessions of a Grieving Christian by Zig Ziglar

Good Grief by Granger E. Westberg

Waiting for Answers: A Parent's Guide to Grief, Resolution and Healing by Betsy Haid

Choosing to See by Mary Beth Chapman

When You Lose Someone You Love by Richard Exley

Finally, if we were limited to only one answer on how we were able to grieve well, it is because of one person. His name is Jesus.

Melanie and I are both born again Christians. At different times in our lives we realized our need for God, repented of our sins and received Jesus Christ into our hearts and lives by faith and were baptized. We are not perfect people. We have a lot to learn and a long way to go, but because we have a personal relationship with our Lord and Savior Jesus Christ, we know He walks with us – even in the deepest darkness.

Jesus has been there to help us and comfort us in ways that are hard to explain unless you know Him. As a Christian couple our faith was of utmost importance in getting us through our hardest days. We realize people have many different beliefs about religion. But we want to humbly ask you to consider the claims of Christ. He was born of a virgin, lived a sinless life, died on the cross to pay the penalty for our sins, and rose again on the third day.

God helped us get through this. He is real. Jesus is a life-changer. If you have not had an encounter with the living Lord, we pray you will put your trust completely in Him.

Truly, truly, I say to you, unless a grain of wheat falls into the earth and dies, it remains alone; but if it dies, it bears much fruit.

JOHN 12:24 (ESV)

18

Fruit

During the visitation for Cooper at Hope Church, hundreds of people visited with Melanie and our girls and me, offering hugs, tears, kind words, and reassurances. Hour after hour, they came – family, friends, church family, AFR listeners and even some local folks who didn't know us but heard about this beautiful little boy's death and were just compelled to offer whatever comfort they could.

Every hour or so during the event, my mentor and close friend Steve Hallman would come alongside and put his arm around me. He'd ask how I was holding up, ask if I needed something to eat or drink, and reiterate how sorry he was for us and our loss.

Then, each time, he'd lean in and whisper in my ear, "God doesn't waste pain. He didn't waste it in the Old Testament, and He didn't waste it in the New Testament." He assured me that even if I didn't understand just yet, the time would come when we would see God use our grief to glorify Himself and to give us deep satisfaction that this all had a reason and a purpose.

I wouldn't recommend his statement as a one-size-fits-all comfort phrase for those in the depths of life-changing loss. But Steve is the reason I moved to Mississippi; he helped me get into radio; he was the minister that married Melanie and me; and he preached at Cooper's graveside service. He had earned the right to talk to me, brother to brother, to remind me that Cooper's death wasn't some meaningless occurrence that happened when God wasn't looking.

Even with the lifelong and trustworthy friendship Steve and I share,

I wasn't able to digest his words just then. Melanie and I each had followed the Lord as much as we knew how for decades, but a few hours into the shock, guilt, and loss of direction that came with losing Cooper, we couldn't muster up the concern even to care whether anyone else was helped or not. We just wanted our baby boy back. Over the months and years since, though, God has shown us just how true Steve's words were.

Cooper's death, as gut-wrenching as the aftermath was and occasionally still is, would be unbearable without the Scriptures that have strengthened Christians for centuries in their days of trouble. Two of the most familiar such passages are in the eighth chapter of Romans: "And we know that all things work together for good to them that love God, to them who are the called according to His purpose" (v. 28), and "For I am persuaded, that neither death, nor life, nor angels, nor principalities, nor powers, nor things present, nor things to come, nor height, nor depth, nor any other creature, shall be able to separate us from the love of God, which is in Christ Jesus our Lord" (v. 38-39).

Early in the message that God gave him, the prophet Joel described the utter devastation of God's people when locusts eat what's left of their drought-ruined crops, and then an enemy overruns the nation. That's an apt description of how our grief felt at times: Parched. Desolate. Destroyed. Vanquished.

But God didn't leave His people in drought and famine and desolation and defeat. He promised a time of plenty and peace when "I will restore to you the years that the swarming locust has eaten" (Joel 2:25).

He didn't leave our family in the devastation of raw grief, either. Eventually, when the thickest part of our fog of emotion lifted, God started showing us how He was using our loss for eternal purposes. Gradually, as we began seeing the fruit that came from Cooper's death – fruit that we could not have imagined on our own – He transformed our grief from mere endurance to something resembling an offering.

Flipped

You've read Lauren's account of how Cooper's death dovetailed with the "Flipped" talk the students had just heard a few hours before, and how they'd been schooled in the reality that "one call can change your life."

When Lauren got that call, and when the camp pastor explained to the kids what had happened, immediately 36 kids came to the altar.

Sit back and soak that in: Within minutes after we'd broken the news to Lauren, Cooper's death had prompted 36 teens to devote their hearts, their lives and their eternities to Jesus.

"It was a wake-up call. God took one to save a lot," one student said. Lauren's uncle Jeremy recalled, "It was genuine. It was a moment that was sealed and stamped. God used tragedy for His triumph."

The irony is not lost on us that God wove together a talk about someone's world being "flipped" just as our world flipped along with that dune buggy.

Flame On

Another fruit God produced from our pain involved the football team at Susan Moore High School, a public school in Alabama, where my friend Steve had become principal. Melanie and I visited Steve and his wife, Sarah, a few months after Cooper's death, and they invited us to the school's football game that night. At their pregame meal Steve had told the football team about Cooper and his "Flame On!" approach to life, tying it to 2 Timothy 1:6, which says, "Fan into flame the gift of God, which is in you." He used both to encourage the students to live life "wide open," as Cooper had.

"Boy, did they take that and run with it!" Steve said later.

The team came out onto the field with "Flame On" written on wrist tape, eye black and other places, and they handily won. Steve took me to the locker room after the game to meet the team. Just before we went in, without their even knowing we were going to be there, we heard them shout in unison, "One, two, three – Flame On!" The seniors adopted "Flame On" as their motto, and Steve said for the rest of that school year, that became a kind of universal encouragement among the students. They even had "Flame On" printed on their senior t-shirts.

We also learned through friends that the tennis team at Pontotoc High School, a public school just a few miles from our home, had adopted the "Flame On" motto as their theme. Coach Kevin Morrow agreed with the student-led effort. They, too, had "Flame On" in big, bold letters along with the Bible reference "2 Timothy 1:6" emblazoned on their team shirts. Coach Morrow told the local newspaper, "A lot of questions were asked about the shirt during the season, and I was proud that the kids would share how they were honoring the death of J.J.'s son, Cooper, and how it motivated them to do their best on the court. It's been a very good theme. It really gave our team a lot of unity and purpose. It's given our kids a lot of opportunities to make a difference for the kingdom of God."

The Documentary

Believing that our story could help other people dealing with tragic loss, Melanie, our girls and I went through the sometimes agonizing, sometimes healing process of reliving on-camera our memories of Cooper's death and beyond. Some wonderfully gifted people took what we shared, added recollections from close friends and insights from ministry leaders like Dr. James Dobson, and created **Flame On**, a 42-minute documentary.

Since then, American Family Association has distributed more than 50,000 copies of the movie, and we've heard back from hundreds of those viewers who have shared the DVD with audiences from their extended families and Sunday school classes to civic clubs. I have personally delivered thousands of copies of the video, including many to people in Australia, Bangladesh and the Dominican Republic. Friends have shared them in other far-off places. Bubba Lollar, then pastor of Kingshurst Evangelical Church in Birmingham, England, told me they promoted the viewing of **Flame On** for many weeks before they showed it on a Sunday night. He said it was well received, and there was not a dry eye in the church. He further explained that there were over 20 countries represented in their congregation. He emphasized how he saw firsthand the impact **Flame On** had in the U.K., offering help and hope to those hurting.

We know that **Flame On** has been aired on TV stations in Korea, India and Jamaica. We have no idea how some of that came about, it's just another reminder that God determines His purposes and carries them out in ways beyond our comprehension.

From overseas and here in the United States, it's been such an encouragement for us to hear from many **Flame On** viewers how understanding our family's struggle and seeing God's gradual healing in us has given them hope for their own recovery.

Another 100,000-plus people have watched it online. We are continually amazed at the ripple effect of the documentary. It can be seen on-line at www.jjjasper.com

Other works

Flame On has also gone on to have a role in other works that God is doing.

Alex and Stephen Kendrick are the brothers who shepherded the film ministry of Sherwood Baptist Church in Albany, Georgia. Under the name Sherwood Pictures the church creates compelling films that present the Gospel of grace while they entertain and inspire, including **Flywheel**, **Facing the Giants**, **Fireproof**, and **Courageous**.

Both Kendrick brothers are American Family Radio listeners. They have supported and promoted our work, and we've helped promote their ministry as well. Several years ago they invited us to come to Albany to do a broadcast on-site where they were filming **Fireproof**, starring Kirk Cameron. We've been friends since.

The Kendrick brothers and other members of the film ministry at Sherwood were already planning their film **Courageous** when mutual friends called to tell them of Cooper's death. After a time they approached us about our experience with tragedy and grief.

"We felt the Lord leading us to deal with certain kinds of grief and then overcome that with a courageous faith, so there's an element in the movie **Courageous** where one of the couples deals with the loss of a child," Alex said. "We very cautiously approached J.J. and asked if we could go through the emotions, the grief that he went through. ... Stephen and I incorporated a lot of what J.J. shared with us into the movie **Courageous** because it was so real, based on real events – horrible events."

"We're very grateful that God has used a tragedy that's going to help us to call men to spiritual leadership in their homes," Stephen said. "And Cooper's story is going to be part of helping us minister to families all over the world."

Both **Flame On** and **Courageous** were nominated for awards at the 2012 San Antonio Independent Christian Film Festival, adding to the audiences that saw the glory of God in the stories they shared. **Flame On** was a semifinalist in the documentary category, and **Courageous** won the "Best of Festival" Jubilee Award.

If I was surprised that Alex and Stephen wanted to incorporate our experiences into their film, I was equally astonished when I got an email from radio producers asking if I would team up with pastor and best-selling author Max Lucado and Sheila Walsh to tape a radio special titled **God's Story, Your Story**. Sheila Walsh is a Scottish-born Christian singer/songwriter, best selling author, featured speaker and television personality who shares her inspiring story of the struggle with depression. The radio special aired nationally on many stations in 2011. In the special, I told Max the lesson about God, that Cooper's death had driven home. "He's completely in charge, completely in control. He hasn't walked away from His post; He's not asleep at the switch. Even when things are going wrong in our life, when the wheels are coming off and things are unraveling, He is a good God. He is faithful, He is sovereign, and He has a plan.

Later Max reached out to us asking permission to use our story in a sermon series he was planning on how the Lord brings His people through incredibly difficult trials.

He also went on to write about Cooper's death and how we've learned to trust God even more completely through it. In his book *You'll Get Through This: Hope and Help for Your Turbulent Times,* he drew parallels between our grief; the battle his wife, Denalyn, had with depression; and the patriarch Joseph's enslavement and false imprisonment.

After noting how Denalyn "found God's presence amid God's people," Max added, "So did J.J. His hurts are still deep, but his faith is deep still. Whenever he tells the story of losing Cooper, he says this: 'We know what the bottom looks like, and we know who is waiting there – Jesus Christ.'" We highly recommend Max Lucado's inspiring book, *You'll Get Through This: Hope and Help for Your Turbulent Times.*

The Cooper Jasper Foundation

Perhaps the greatest fear of someone grieving is that their loved one will be forgotten or that somehow their life did not have an impact and was not meaningful.

We established the Cooper Jasper Foundation to help people in Cooper's name and honor his memory. The Lord has blessed us to be able to give gifts to Christian schools, pregnancy resource centers and global missions work. We have given small scholarships in Cooper's honor to help students pay college tuition. We have used some of the funds to purchase additional **Flame On** DVDs to continue making them available at no charge. These are a few of the ways people are helped through the foundation. The foundation is a Mississippi non-profit corporation and donations to the Cooper Jasper Foundation are tax deductible.[8]

Another fruit from Cooper's death is opportunities for Melanie to share our story publicly. While I have breakfast with several hundred thousand listeners every morning, she has always been a private person. But what we've endured and learned since Cooper's death has opened the door for her to speak at Bible studies and at several women's conferences to share God's faithfulness with other hurting people.

Probably the most gratifying ministry that comes with being believers who've lost a child is the opportunity to comfort others who are going through their own gut-wrenching grief. Whether by letter or email, in a phone conversation or face to face, we've had the privilege many times since Cooper's death to help fulfill 2 Corinthians 1:3-4 – "Praise be to the God and Father of our Lord Jesus Christ, the Father of compassion and the God of all comfort, who comforts us in all our troubles, so that we can comfort those in any trouble with the comfort we ourselves receive from God."

When Cooper died, we saw the body of Christ in action. Some friends came and stayed with us the first several nights, making themselves available around the clock. Others took care of our girls, helping both them and us to get through the first days of crisis. Countless people called, emailed, sent cards, and visited. We felt the prayers of hundreds of thousands of people in the American Family Radio audience, and that made an incredible difference in our life by holding us up.

After a tragedy or death the shock and loss is so great that our immediate response is often, "This is a total loss." The scorched earth, ground zero effect leads us to believe that it's hopeless and no good can possibly come from this bad situation. Many things are impossible with men, but with God all things are possible! Though we were tempted to think, *Not even God can bring good from this horrible tragedy,* we were mistaken. We are witnesses to how good and great God truly is. He can take the worst mistake, failure, or even death and someway, somehow glorify Himself and even create new life from it.

Melanie and I are amazed at how Cooper's story has been used in sermons, books and movies. Many people have told us personally how Cooper's life inspired them.

All four Gospel writers tell us that Jesus used five loaves and two fishes from one little boy to feed more than five thousand people. Melanie and I take satisfaction in the idea that the life of our little boy might reach five million with some portion of the good news that comes from the God of all comfort.

If you're reading this, you're almost certainly dealing with your own profound pain or sharing someone else's. Let us assure you that your suffering is not random or meaningless.

We only have to look as far as the cross to know what my friend Steve told me is true: God doesn't waste pain.

May the God of hope fill you with all joy and peace as you trust in him, so that you may overflow with hope by the power of the Holy Spirit.

ROMANS 15:13

19

Hope

On a short term mission trip to Dhaka, Bangladesh, we quickly discovered that the game cricket is loved by nearly everyone there. Cricket fans seemed to be as fanatical as U.S. sports fans.

On this particular day, the Bangladesh Tigers were playing Sri Lanka and it was causing quite a buzz. Our hosts tried their best to explain the game of cricket to us but the learning curve was too steep. Throughout the day, everywhere we went, everyone was talking about the "big game." We were visiting a slum in Dhaka and even with the language barrier we could tell the locals were excitedly chattering about the match. I asked our interpreter, "How's the game going? What's the score?"

With a wide grin he said Sri Lanka is ahead 198 to 0! My expression must have revealed what I was thinking because he quickly added, "Oh, not to worry, we haven't been up to bat yet!" Talk about a glass half full attitude! Even at 198 to 0 everyone around us in that far away land was smiling, optimistic and full of hope.

The need for hope is universal isn't it? If you are suffering or grieving or experiencing some sort of setback perhaps it feels like the score is 198 to 0. Be encouraged, there is hope. If your struggle is in the very raw stages you may not believe it or even want to hear it, but help is on the way. The dark clouds will eventually part to let rays of sunshine peek through. As God allows time to pass, the awful suffocating waves that crash over you will be more spaced out. Believe me you will even laugh again one day. Joy will overtake you and your good days will outnumber the bad ones. Better days are ahead. The windshield is bigger than the rear view mirror.

Please trust me on this. I couldn't imagine things ever getting better when I was given that same encouragement at our lowest point, but it's true. God will make a way where there is no way. He was with Shadrach, Meshach, and Abednego in the fiery furnace. He was with Daniel in the lion's den, He was with Joseph in the pit, and He will be there for you. Against all hope, Abraham in hope, believed God. Even with all the circumstances against him, Abraham gave glory to God declaring that God was able to do what He had promised.

If things look bleak and seemingly hopeless from your vantage point, allow me to declare with the enthusiasm of a Bangladesh cricket fan – your team hasn't stepped up to bat yet. God will send family, friends and church members to your aid. It will seem like the cavalry is coming over the hill to your rescue. God has people you don't even know who love you and are praying for you. And He will find ways to minister to your heart quietly, to remind you that He loves you, He is with you and you are precious in His sight.

I know what it is like to grieve and miss someone you love. There are many things I miss about Cooper. I miss how tightly he snuggled into me while we would sit on the couch watching TV. I miss our special father and son times working around the farm. I miss hearing him laugh and those amazing hugs of his. I miss how he smelled after he had been playing hard. "You smell like a puppy dog," Melanie would often say. There are hundreds of little things about him I miss, like how he would rub his fingers across the ridges on my thumbnail, a habit he had when he sat beside me. I miss how, when he was small, he would absentmindedly reach over to touch my face and rub my chin while we sat together. I miss how excitedly he would run to the door expectantly when he heard my truck coming up the driveway. There are so many things I miss about Cooper. Things that others wouldn't notice or even care about. Yes, they're little things but things I desperately miss about that amazing little fellow I called Coop.

It's a hopeless feeling knowing we will never hold our little boy, hear him laugh or watch him play ever again until we see him in heaven. We will never celebrate another birthday with him or have the privilege of tucking him into bed. That realization causes a sadness and depression to settle in like a blanket of fog on a cold bleak winter day. It's a feeling of hopelessness. In the first hours, weeks and months after Cooper's death we were numb and just milled around in a zombie-like state. I remember on several occasions walking into a corner store, forgetting what I went in to buy and just standing there having a "Cooper moment." After several minutes in a trance I would be interrupted by the store clerk's voice which seemed to be way off in the distance. As the clerk's voice got clearer, I would snap out of it to hear them say, "Sir, are you all right? Do I need to call someone for you? Are you okay?"

It was all we could do to just put one foot in front of the other. The unthinkable had happened – every parent's worst nightmare. Someone has suggested that there is no greater pain on the planet than losing a child. I agree. All pain is real and I surely wouldn't want to minimize how anyone is hurting, but having a child die is different. I've had lots of time to reflect on it and have concluded that with our parents or grandparents we see subtle signs of aging. They get gray hair or they may miss a step here and there, and while you don't dare dwell on it, you have many hints over a lifetime to know that dreadful day is coming. Your elderly loved ones are going to die. So you at least get to mentally prepare for it even if it's subconsciously.

Regarding the death of a child, there's not even a category in your brain for that. You just don't go there. If there was any possibility in your thinking that your child would be here today but gone tomorrow you couldn't function. You surely would never let them ride a bike, jump on a trampoline or learn to swim. You would never let them out of your sight. Parents aren't supposed to outlive their children. It seems unnatural and out of order.

For me personally if you took all of the pain and disappointment accrued in my entire lifetime and wadded it all up, it wouldn't even be a down payment on the pain I felt after Cooper died. I really can't describe the anguish that seemed to scream from every cell of my body, the ache and longing just to hold our son one more time. To hold him and kiss him and hear his voice. Often I would come home and find Melanie in Cooper's room on his bed curled up in a fetal position, sobbing.

That's how we felt early on: helpless and without hope. Even knowing that God is real and He loves us, the pain still competed with our faith in God and often got the best of us.

Since Cooper's death we have met dozens of others who have lost loved ones, and the number one ingredient they're starving for is hope. That is certainly common among parents who have had a child die. I remember the email from a Georgia man whose son had killed himself. He was hopeless. Then there was the desperate call we received about a sweet man who was sleep deprived and under tremendous stress; and in that distracted state, instead of dropping his toddler off at daycare he left the baby in the car seat in the vehicle on a hot summer day. Or the couple that reached out to us when they laid their baby in the crib only to discover the next morning the baby had died of SIDS. We spent many hours praying and crying with that sweet couple. I could tell you the details about the coach whose son took his life in the tree house in their back yard, but it would be too painful. In these stories and others like them, the one thing they all desperately needed was hope.

You may have heard it said, "We can go many days without food, several days without water, and even moments without oxygen, but we can't survive without hope." God has made mankind sturdy and resilient. We can rebound against seemingly insurmountable odds. We can bounce back from disappointment, trials, tribulations, health concerns, financial set backs, heartaches, and even the death of a loved one – if we don't lose hope. Without hope we give up completely.

Years ago I attended a Bible study where the teacher was emphasizing the importance of God's Word. He explained how the Bible is the inspired, inerrant and living Word of God. He stressed the importance of reading the Bible in context rather than skipping around reading one or two obscure verses here and there. He challenged us to read an entire chapter to see what God was teaching there. Or to read an entire book in the Bible, then step back and see what the theme for that book was.

That night, when at home, I heeded the teacher's advice. I flipped open my Bible and it landed on Mark chapter five in the New Testament. I read the entire chapter. Sometimes portions of the Bible have several wise sayings, a story or precepts and principles. I quickly noticed in this chapter, however, that there are only three stories. The story of a demon possessed man, a sick woman, and a young girl who had died. In the story of the demon possessed man it says, "For he had often been chained hand and foot but he tore the chains apart and broke the irons on his feet" (Mark 5:4). No one was strong enough to subdue him. This was a serious problem. The townspeople did all they could with their resources but to no avail. Jesus arrived on the scene and saved the day.

The second story is about a sick woman. In vv. 25-26 it says, "And a woman was there who had been subject to bleeding for 12 years. She had suffered a great deal under the care of many doctors and had spent all she had, yet instead of getting better she grew worse." How discouraging. Here was a woman with a health concern that she had suffered with for 12 long years, day in and day out. She was desperate to get relief. She obviously got referrals, went to many doctors and spent all her money in the process. If she at least felt the same after her odyssey she would have at least broken even. But she felt worse, adding insult to injury. Then she heard about Jesus, sought Him out, touched the hem of His garment, and was completely healed!

Next there was a young girl who had died. Surely this would be the time to give up hope, except nothing is impossible with God. Jesus raised her from the dead.

Three stories of hopelessness. Someone trapped by demonic power is very serious. It affected the entire village. They did all they knew to do but without success – until Jesus arrived! Same with the sick lady. No hope. In fact, as hard as she tried, her situation went from bad to worse – until Jesus arrived! Then she experienced a breakthrough. We know how much pain and suffering engulfed the family whose daughter died. But Jesus provided hope and healing.

The message in the fifth chapter of Mark is clear to me. Three stories where people seemingly had no hope. Three situations completely out of control. They exhausted every avenue humanly possible but without remedy. The hero in the story is Jesus. It's not over until God says it's over. He gets the last word. He has the last say. Maybe you think your marriage is over. Perhaps you're struggling with a health concern or, like us, you have had a loved one die. God offers hope through Jesus Christ our Lord. As bleak as things may look I'm convinced that God gave us an entire chapter in the Bible to trumpet the good news that even when it seems helpless and hopeless, Jesus can help. Jesus is the hero in our story. That's why we're still standing. God has helped and sustained us throughout our difficulties. We have sensed His presence throughout our journey and if you will allow Him He will help you and give you hope. Jesus can be the hero of your story.

The goal of this book is to tell our story, honor our son's memory and glorify the Lord. We want to help others grieve well and offer hope. Ultimate hope comes through a personal relationship with Jesus Christ.

In the April 2011 *AFA Journal*, pastor Don Locke wrote:

Because Christ rose from the dead if you have received Him as Savior, you are a child of God. Scripture assures us that "to all who did receive Him, who believed in His name, He gave the right to become children of God" (John 1:12, ESV).

In the resurrection Jesus defeated death, not only for Himself, but for every child of God. Because of that, the day of your death is not the end of life, but the door to eternal life – a great day of homecoming. Because of the resurrection, the child of God can face even death itself with the assurance of God's care and with the assurance that he will experience indescribable joy in the presence of our Savior for all of eternity.

This provides great comfort not only as we contemplate our own death, but also when a close friend or family member dies and we know they had trusted Jesus as Savior. Oh yes, we will grieve, but not like those who have no hope because we know that they have gone home. Not only that, but we know that we will see them again when we go home.[9]

Thank you for reading this book. We hope the Lord used it to encourage and inspire you. Please contact us if we can pray for you.[10] It would be our privilege to pray for you like others did for us. Prayer is the difference maker! In fact, we have already prayed for you. Our family prayed for those who would read this book who have suffered loss to not be paralyzed by grief and depression. We prayed for you to have strength and to be comforted by the One who loves you most:

> "For God so loved the world, that He gave His only begotten Son, that whosoever believeth in Him should not perish, but have everlasting life" (John 3:16 KJV).

Our prayer for you is to grieve well with God's help. God loves you, and so do we – Flame on!

Notes

Chapter 1: Suddenly

1. Mary Beth Chapman with Ellen Vaughn, *Choosing to See* (Grand Rapids, MI: Revell, 2010), p.19.

2. Max Lucado, *You'll Get Through This* (Nashville, TN: Thomas Nelson, Inc., 2013), p. 3.

Chapter 4: Pro-Life

3. Steve Farrar, *Point Man* (USA: Multnomah Publishers, Inc., 1990, 2003), p. 176, 177, 179, 180.

Chapter 12: Guilt and Regret

4. "Grace for a Lifetime" lyrics. Paul S. Chapman/Times & Seasons Music/BMI used with permission. For entire song lyrics visit **www. steveandanniechapman.com.**

Chapter 13: Forgiveness

5. Paul L. Tan, *Encyclopedia of 15,000 Illustrations: Signs of the Times* (Bible Communications, Inc., 1998).

Chapter 15: Flame On

6. American Family Association (AFA), a non-profit 501(c)(3) organization, was founded in 1977 by Donald E. Wildmon. Since 1977, AFA has been on the frontlines of America's culture war. The original name of the ministry was National Federation For Decency but was

changed to American Family Association in 1988. Today, AFA is one of the largest and most effective pro-family organizations in the country with over two million online supporters and approximately 155,000 paid subscribers to the *AFA Journal*, the ministry's monthly magazine. In addition, AFA owns and operates nearly 200 radio stations across the country under the American Family Radio (AFR) banner. Other divisions of AFA include the AFA Foundation; OneNewsNow.com, an online news provider that is syndicated around the world; and American Family Studios, AFA's film and video arm.

Chapter 17: Grieving Well

7. Betsy Haid, *Waiting for Answers* (Sisters, OR: Deep River Books 2010) pp. 124-125

Chapter 18: Fruit

8. The Cooper Jasper Foundation is a Mississippi non-profit corporation that is operated strictly for religious, educational, and charitable purposes and donations to the foundation are tax deductible under IRS rules. Donations can be sent to the Cooper Jasper Foundation, P. O. Drawer 2440, Tupelo, MS 38803.

Chapter 19: Hope

9. Don Locke, pastor, Houston Presbyterian Church (PCA), Houston, Mississippi.

10. Contact us at P. O. Box 804, Tupelo, MS 38802 or at **www.jjjasper. com** or on social media.